To Clive

with Great love

+ Thanks for everything

— dream included.!!

lain

May '95

DREAMWORK, ANTHROPOLOGY AND THE CARING PROFESSIONS

For my Mother and Father

Dreamwork, Anthropology and the Caring Professions

A cultural approach to dreamwork

IAIN R. EDGAR PhD
Senior Lecturer in Social Work
Department of Social Work and Social Policy
University of Northumbria
Newcastle upon Tyne

Avebury

Aldershot · Brookfield USA · Hong Kong · Singapore · Sydney

Published by
Avebury
Ashgate Publishing Limited
Gower House
Croft Road
Aldershot
Hants GU11 3HR
England

Ashgate Publishing Company
Old Post Road
Brookfield
Vermont 05036
USA

British Library Cataloguing in Publication Data

Edgar, Iain R.
    Dreamwork, Anthropology and the Caring
    Professions: Cultural Approach to Dreamwork
    I. Title
    154.634
 ISBN 1-85628-526-X

Library of Congress Catalog Card Number: 94-74550

Printed and bound by Athenæum Press Ltd.,
Gateshead, Tyne & Wear.

Contents

Acknowledgements

I should like to thank all those who have contributed to this book. The book has developed out of a PhD research project into the social anthropology of dreamwork in the UK. My supervisor for my PhD was Professor Ronnie Frankenberg of Keele University Department of Sociology and Social Anthropology, to whom I am most grateful for his initial and continuing encouragement and advice. The late David Brooks, formerly of the Department of Anthropology at Durham University, was an inspiring influence on the development of my thesis, particularly with respect to the value and role of ritual process. I am grateful to Judith Okely for her invitation to give a paper on anthropology and dreaming at the 1989 Association of Social Anthropology Annual Conference which encouraged me to think of developing my initial ideas further. Likewise I am grateful to Kirsten Hastrup and Peter Hervik for their invitation to give a paper on my work at the 1992 European Association of Social Anthropology Conference, and to Suzette Heald for her inclusion of that paper in 'Anthropology and Psychoanalysis' published by Routledge. These events were crucial to the development of my thesis and therefore to this book. A group of fellow social anthropologists have played a supportive and very valuable part in the development of my anthropological ideas through the years and I should like to thank them all. They are: Jean Collins, Jenny Hockey, Allison James, Marie Johnson, Tamara Kohn, Peter Phillimore, Andrew Russell, Bob Simpson, Sue Wright and Malcolm Young. Thanks are also due to Carlotta Johnson for her reading of an early draft of the manuscipt.

I would like to thank particularly my colleagues in the Department of Social Work and Social Policy at the University of Northumbria, at Newcastle, for covering my sabbatical leave which enabled me to write up my thesis. Special thanks are due to Richard Barker for his continuous encouragement, interest and proof-reading, and to Andy Bilson for his great help with the preparation of the camera ready copy. I am also grateful to the University of Northumbria for their financial support towards the preparation of this book.

The members of the dreamwork groups remain anonymous, but clearly without them and their general support and encouragement, this book would not exist. Whilst the intrusion of a rather noisy tape-recorder was occasionally irritating, members were generally content to share their dreams and their lives in the knowledge that such information was potentially part of a research project, as well as a group process. Lastly, many thanks are due to my family for their good humoured support, and particularly to my wife, Anna, for her help with both proof-reading and editing.

Preface

This book combines recent developments in the study of the understanding
of dreams in the fields of social anthropology and psychology to present a
novel cultural approach to dreamwork for those in the caring professions.
Based on a recent ethnographic study of author-led dreamwork groups in
the UK, the book develops an analysis of dreams as a form of culturally-
specific metaphorical thought, and shows how group members made 'sense'
out of the 'nonsense' of dream imagery. Their 'sense' was developed through
experiential groupwork methods such as gestalt, psychodrama and
imagework, and was derived from the language of metaphor and a political,
often feminist, analysis of life events. The book reviews the current use of
dreamwork by the caring professions in such diverse fields as work with the
teminally ill, refugees and children. The book will appeal both to those in
caring professions and also to social anthropologists in the fields of
psychological and medical anthropology.

Iain R. Edgar

Introduction

The central premise of this book is that, irrespective of whether dreams are meaningful in any final sense, people and societies often do find them meaningful. The aim of this book is to develop a synthesis of social anthropological and psychoanalytical approaches to the understanding of dream imagery in UK culture. Based on a recent ethnographic study of author-led dreamwork groups in the UK, the book develops an analysis of dreams as a form of culturally-specific metaphorical thought and shows how group members made 'sense' out of the 'nonsense' of dream imagery. Their 'sense' was developed through experiential groupwork methods such as gestalt, psychodrama and imagework, and was derived from the language of metaphor and a political, often feminist, analysis of life events. More specifically the book has the following detailed aims:

1 To explore the potential value of using dream and fantasy material in practical work with a wide variety of client and group situations.
2 To illustrate the historical development of dreamwork in its various religious and sociological forms.
3 To present an integration of different perspectives on dreaming, drawing on classical and contemporary perspectives in both social anthropology and psychology.
4 To review the current situation with respect to the use of day and night imagery in the caring professions.
5 To provide an overview of methods of working with dreams, such as with gestalt, imagework and psychodrama.
6 To present the findings of my own research into how group members have understood their dream imagery in relation to their current life experience.
7 To develop an innovative and culturally based theory of how dream imagery may be understood in relation to the symbolic construction of contemporary idiomatic language use.

1

8 To develop a ritual and processual analysis of meaning-making within the group context.

9 To develop a perspective, derived from social constructionism, as to how dreamwork can be both a consciousness-raising method which challenges structural oppressions, as well as being significant as a means of personal growth.

10 To consider the way forward in relation to using dreamwork in this field.

This book is primarily intended to be of interest to the following groups of people: workers in the caring professions, such as social workers, counsellors, nurses and doctors who are interested in developing skills and knowledge about understanding and working with their clients' dream material; social anthropologists whose fields include psychological anthropology, the anthropology of consciousness and medical anthropology; anyone interested in dreamwork per se.

The literature of dreamwork

The potential literature on dreaming is vast. A recent two volume encyclopedia of works on dreaming by Nancy Parsifal-Charles (1986) summarised hundreds of books on dreaming through the ages. Social anthropology has studied the dream in its ethnographic context since the work of Tylor (1871) in the C19, and a summary of developments in that subject is included in this book. Recently Tedlock et al (Tedlock, 1987a) have developed a communicative theory of dreaming which integrates psychological and social anthropological perspectives. Sociology began to be interested in dreaming in the 1960's with the work of Bastide (1966), and more recently a session at the American Sociology Association (1990) was devoted to the developing area of the sociology of dreaming. The attempt to understand the significance of the dream has been fundamental to the development of psychoanalytic psychology throughout this century. The work of pioneers such as Jung and Freud is well known, yet that of more recent theorists such as Glucksman and Warner (1987) is not so well known in the caring professions.

In the caring professions there is beginning to be a consideration of using dream imagery as part of assessment and intervention strategies. For instance Buckholz (1990) has described his use of dreams in family therapy; while Malon (1989) and Smith (1990) have begun to explore their value in social casework/clinical work. A North American researcher, Wunder (1990), has very interestingly shown the value of using day and night imagery as both a method of research and as an assessment tool in work with different client groups. Her work focussed on analysing common themes and preoccupations in the mental life, as shown by day and night dreaming, of siblings of children with severe learning difficulties. In

2

chapter four I review the current use of dreamwork in the caring professions. There is currently a plethora of general books of the 'how to explore your dreams type'. These range from the crass to the interesting. Particularly, the works of Montague Ullman (1979 &1989) provide many interesting directions and illustrations of using dreams in the group context. Shohet (1985) has written about the use of dreamwork groups in schools and community settings, as well as the use of dreams for specific consciousness raising purposes such as overcoming racial prejudice. The women's movement particularly has explored the potential contribution of the dream and the products of active imagination (Ernst and Goodison, 1981) with a view to developing a deeper understanding of female personal and social identity.

Distinctive contribution of this book

As I have already indicated it is timely for a book to appear on the subject of using day and night imagery (dreaming) for the caring professions. The value of such dreamwork is currently obscured by the contradictory and polarised evaluations of dreaming. On the one hand 'interpreting dreams' is seen as a highly specialised task reserved for psychoanalysts and needing a long and challenging training. On the other hand, dreaming is denigrated as being wholly illusory, as being just a 'dream' and of no consequence. Dreaming is a universal aspect of being human. It appears to be the most private and hidden activity which is usually perceived as being both unpredictable and often incomprehensible. Yet most human societies have sought to understand dream imagery and many have accorded such imagery and its interpretations high, even prophetic, significance. Mediating this dichotomy is, of course, a substantial popular interest in dream material and there are numerous tabloid newspaper features on 'the meaning of dreams'. Dream images are seen as directly translatable into typical meanings and there are many 'dream dictionaries' (i.e. Gonzalez-Wippler, 1989). Indeed a popular culture of dream interpretation is evident throughout historical times in many societies as Parsifal-Charles (1986) shows in her encyclopaedic and historical review of writing about dream interpretation through the ages. Moreover the concept of the dream and its metaphorical use is widespread in English speaking contemporary society. We refer to the 'dream' as being a normative feature of each of the stages of life. The 'dreams' of youth are contrasted with the disillusion, cynicism and 'lost dreams' of old age. The 'dream' of the 'good life' is seen as a fundamental dynamic in both the construction of human ambition and in the development of a shared social contract. Recently a journalist wrote of how 'goals are just dreams with feet on them' (Observer review, 28.8.94). Social dreams are embedded in human institutions. We dream of 'getting on'; of being carefree and fulfilled in our relationships; of 'falling in love' and so sharing 'love's dream'. Popular music pours out a continuous repertoire of dream

3

references usually about romantic love of the ilk 'I'm dreaming of you!' and its endless, perhaps repetitive, cycle of hope and loss. Societies can be founded on dreams as is the case with the 'American dream' and provide a form of charter myth (Malinowski 1954, p.116). The well known *dreamtime* of Australian aboriginal groups fundamentally constructs their cosmological world-view and social structure. Religious thought, in general, is imbued with anticipatory, visionary hope of the life to come, and the imagery of the consequences of moral choice. Indeed the current situation regarding the evaluation of dream in Westernised societies is even more perplexing when we try to differentiate between vision and dream. Whereas a 'dream' can be discounted as 'just a dream'; a 'vision', whether that of the leader or manager, is highly regarded as a core ability. Sometimes there is even a conflation of these two terms as when Martin Luther King started his famous final speech by saying: 'I have a dream....' Such examples well illustrate our social ambivalence about mental imagery, 'the pictures in our mind'. In short we are both individually and socially replete with socially constructed imagery in which the notion of the dream is a fundamental feature in our collective formation of anticipated futures, and remembered or imagined pasts.

This book will develop a middle way between these polarities. Working with recent theoretical material from both social anthropology and psychology I will show how the 'revised psychoanalytic approach' in psychology has re-evaluated the explicit problem solving function of dreams, and how the study of dreams in their ethnographic context allows us to develop a sophisticated analysis of the social construction of dream imagery and its meaning in Western society. I will describe how the dreamwork movement, derived from the particular social context of the U.S.A. in the 1960s and 1970s, has developed approaches and methods of working with dream imagery that allow professionals to work productively with such rich material. I will show, through my analysis of dreamwork groups that I have both led and studied, that dreams offer a direct route into accessing the key concerns and dilemmas of both individuals and groups. The relationship between current life events and dream imagery will be explored and amply illustrated by interesting and original case material.

I will present a novel way of interpreting dreams that shows how dream imagery constitutes metaphors of the self whose interpretation can be derived through a consideration of symbolic meaning embedded in ordinary language use. A further innovative approach in this book is an analysis of the cultural specificity of dream imagery and its associated interpretive paradigms. Of particular interest will be the contextualisation of dream interpretation in current Western society whereby the impact of structural approaches to the understanding of the self in society influence interpretation. For instance, feminism has significantly critiqued and re-evaluated the position of women in society and such a perspective affects our understanding of stereotypes as represented in dream imagery. This book also intends to link, theoretically and practically, link with the new

4

therapies of psychosynthesis and transpersonal psychology (Assagioli, 1980).

Chapter one: the dream in history

This chapter will focus on the place of dreamwork within some of of the main religious traditions. Dream interpretation has traditionally had a strong basis in many religious traditions. Dreaming has been, and is still in part, seen by some of the great religions as a core means of communication between God and his/her people. The role of the dream in Christian, Judaic and Baha'i society will be introduced. To illustrate the historical evaluation of dreamwork, I will focus on the place of the dream in Islamic tradition, since particular significance is accorded to dreaming in that tradition (Gouda, 1991). I consider briefly Islamic classificatory systems and dream lexicons and consider a sociological reflection on the political as well as personal interpretations of dreams. I link the Islamic theory of 'imaginal thought' to the Jungian method of active imagination as it is currently being used and developed in the new therapies of psychosynthesis and transpersonal psychology.

Chapter two: psychological approaches to dreamwork

In this chapter I present the classic psychoanalytic theories on the nature of the unconscious and the role of dreams in relation to everyday life. I give particular attention to the Freudian distinction between primary and secondary thinking and between manifest and latent content. I consider Jung's theory of the archetypes and the collective unconscious along with his compensation theory of dreaming. I describe Jung's development of the practice of active imagination. I introduce the theory and practice of transpersonal psychology. I consider contemporary neo-Freudian approaches, particularly the 'revised psychoanalytic approach' (Glucksman and Warner, 1987), which has re-evaluated Freud's distinction between primary and secondary process thinking and between manifest and latent meaning. This approach sees dreaming as an integrative and problem-solving function of the mind which utilises a metaphorical form of thinking characteristic of dream imagery. I also discuss Perl's Gestalt theory of dreaming and dream interpretation.

Chapter three: the social anthropological perspective

The aim of this chapter is to show how dream material is socially constructed in specific and very different societies. This perspective will then inform our awareness of the value of dream material in Western industrialised societies. While I will introduce particular examples of the role, function and use of dreams in societies studied by social anthropologists, my main focus will be on the development of social anthropological theory with regard to dreaming, rather than providing 'exotic' vignettes of dream usage in third world societies. I will briefly review the historical develoment of theory beginning with the work of Tylor and Rivers in the C19. I will continue with a consideration of the influence of Freudian perspectives in the 1920s and 30s. The work of Seligman (Seligman, 1923) and his search for 'Type dreams',which intended to show universal latent meaning in dreams across all societies, was determined by Freudian theory. Likewise I will note Lincoln's (Lincoln, 1935) work on the distinction between 'individual' and 'culture pattern' dreams. I describe the 'content analysis' approach of the 1950s and 60's to the study of dreams, which attempted to quantify and cross-culturally analyse dream imagery in order to show patterns of cultural and personality variables.

I continue with the development of ethnopsychiatry in the 1950s by Devereux (Devereux, 1966) and his concept of the pathogenic dream. The cross-cultural work of D'Andrade (D'Andrade,1961), the conflict-resolution approach of Crapanzano (Crapanzano, 1975), and the structuralist attempts of Kuper (Kuper, 1979) to compare the logic of myths with that of dream material will be briefly surveyed. Finally I present the recent work of Tedlock et al and their development of a new communicative theory of dreaming, in which the traditional boundary between the psychology and anthropology of dreaming is redefined. Their communicative theory of dream analysis proposes as the object of study the consideration of the dream as a communicative event that involves the creative dynamics of narration; a study of the psychodynamic and cultural aspects of the group setting; and the indigenous dream theories of the society.

Chapter four: the dream and the caring professions

I start this chapter with a fuller discussion of the potential use of dream material in a variety of care settings, ranging from counselling to groupwork and to family therapy settings. Thereafter I will consider the current position in relation to the use of dream and daytime imagery, particularly in recent work with terminally ill people, people with learning difficulties and with refugees. I will also explore the potential use of dreamwork in supervision and team-building.

Chapter five: methods of working with dreams

This chapter is a methods chapter and will draw on the work of several dreamwork practitioners as well as on the author's own experience. Whilst I do not adopt a manual type approach to the description of methods such as gestalt, psychodrama, meditation, artwork and guided fantasy, I aim to show through the use of case-material how these methods amplify the meaning-making potential of narrated dream imagery. I will describe concepts such as dream amplification and dialoguing in user-friendly ways. I will show how to use the power of the group as an enabling force in dream exploration. I will discuss how to structure dreamwork groups as well as ways of working with spontaneous dream disclosures in various settings.

Chapter six: the group

This chapter focuses on the group context and examines its dynamic process and how this process interacted with the dreamwork. In particular I consider the following: characteristics of the members; the stages of the group; decision-making and leadership; conflict and communication; trust and self-disclosure and members evaluation of the group. Overall in this chapter I analyse the social dynamics of the dream sharing which Tedlock's communicative theory of dreaming proposes as an essential aspect of anthropological analysis, and which I suggest is equally important as a factor in dreamwork practice.

Chapter seven: metaphor, ritual and language

A striking development in understanding dreams was developed by the groups I was involved in. Members often came to 'make sense' of their dream imagery through a group exploration of social meaning embedded in linguistic metaphor. An example of this is a dream situation in which the female dreamer is going for a job interview carrying a loaf with icing on it which suddenly started to drip off. Overall the dream was finally understood by her as reflecting her anxiety and fear of assessment linked to a present fragility of self image in the domestic sphere. However, throughout the discussion and gestalt exercise, which involved her identifying with the icing on the bread, a powerful theme for the group was the spontaneous discovery of the various metaphorical uses of bread in ordinary language use, such as 'using your loaf', being kneaded'. 'being proved', 'being good enough to eat', a 'bun in the oven' and 'loafing about'. Whilst these were humorous asides they also constituted sometimes powerful metaphorical summaries of the dreamer's self-state. She, during this session, developed an identification with the bread symbol which became a multi-vocal symbol of the self capable of many different amplifications of meaning, all of which are based on the dialogue between self and group, image and idiomatic discourse. My material contains several vivid such examples of such attribution of meaning, via the connection with idiomatic language use, to dream imagery. Interestingly, such a process of meaning construction shows clearly the interaction of psyche and society and illustrates the social construction of the deepest levels of the unconscious.

Chapter eight: the social construction of the unconscious and its implications

Leading on from the work of the preceding chapter, this chapter will further develop the concept of the cultural or social construction of the unconscious and the implication of this theory for working with personal and social imagery. The value of presenting ethnographic material and the importance of understanding the cultural context of dreaming and dreamwork will become clear as we see that dream imagery is necessarily located in a particular social as well as personal context. Hence, dream data contains highly socially constructed data which can be utilised for consciousness raising purposes as well as for personal growth work. Ullman (1989) has for instance discussed how a sociological or anthropological perspective on dreaming can unmask prevailing personal and group myths and stereotypes about men and women and black and white people. Lawrence (1989) has coined the term 'social dreaming' to articulate the potential value of the dream as a form of social critique, exemplified in Beradt's study of how people dreamt in Nazi Germany in the 1930s. Dreams then are powerful reservoirs of current social and group meanings and potential awarenesses, which can be utilised for personal and social change in the group context.

Chapter nine: conclusion

The conclusion considers both the social anthropological implications of the study as well as summarising the value and potential use of dreamwork for the caring professions.

Case-studies

Throughout this book I will illustrate and develop the points I am making by reference to the groups that I co-led and studied. It is important then to introduce the groups studied at this point so as to provide contextual information for the benefit of the reader. A fuller discussion of the groups is the focus of chapter six. The genesis of these dreamwork groups and the associated research lies in my own long standing interest and occasional 'use' of my own personal dream imagery. For over twenty years I have often been struck by the ability of dream imagery to reformulate imaginatively situations that were preoccupying my waking thoughts. These reformulations, although often bizarre, sometimes seemed to have an anticipatory aspect to them rather as Basso (1987, p.101) has suggested. I found that occasionally by dwelling on a seemingly powerful dream image and by turning it around in my mind and considering how it might relate to developing situations in my life I was able to arrive at a conclusion. Such a conclusion often took the form of a decision about the direction of my life with respect to for instance career development or relationship issues. I then considered that the process I was conducting was a more explicit formulation of the folk wisdom to 'sleep on it' if one had a difficult problem to mull over. So for several years I kept a dream diary and consciously tried to remember my dreams. At this time I immersed myself in the work of Jung and realised that he had similarily advocated such a significant relationship to one's dream imagery. By significant he meant that it was insufficient to relate to dream imagery solely as a kind of internalised source of artwork but that through a dialogue with one's dream imagery important insights might emerge that could lead to personal change and development.

This off and on personal interest developed in two ways. Firstly, I encountered the dreamwork movement in the mid 1980s through participation as a member in a personal development group that included a consideration of dreams. This particular group combined bodywork exercises, meditation and discussion of members' dream imagery. The dreamwork movement itself began in the 1970s in the U.S.A. as an offshoot of the human potential or personal growth movement. At this time the publication of works by authors such as Garfield (1974) and Ullman and Zimmerman (1979) both popularised and guided groups and individuals into ways of working with their dreams. The dreamwork movement values dream imagery as being of potential benefit to the dreamer and the 'meaning' of such imagery as being accessible and understandable to the interested person (Hillman, 1989). Dreamwork groups are relatively commonplace in the U.S.A. but are less frequent in the U.K. Through the group that I participated in I became interested in the linking of group process to the understanding of dream material. Secondly, whilst researching a therapeutic community (Edgar, 1986) I experienced a significant sequence of dreams just before, during and after the fieldwork stage. I found that contemplating these images and wondering how they might relate to the fieldwork experience was a powerful source of insight development, and assisted in my orientation to the varying stages of the fieldwork process and imaginatively prefigured core themes of my research (Edgar, 1989).

The publication of Tedlock's edited volume on contemporary anthropological approaches to dreamwork both re-established the cultural analysis of dreamwork as part of the anthropological enterprise and also showed me that there was a dearth of data about the cultural aspects of dreamwork in advanced industrial societies. Then, at the same time, it became evident from my contacts that there were a number of people who had an interest in dreaming and in interpreting dream imagery in a group context. The idea of establishing a dreamwork group thus had a dual aim:

both to facilitate dream interpretation in a group context for therapeutic purposes and, at the same time, to study this process.

The dreamwork groups

The main experience of dreamwork groups that I will be drawing on consists of co-leading three ten week groups of approximately two to two and a half hours duration. These happened between September 1989 and June 1990. Recruitment to the group was by local advertising, word of mouth and through the membership networks of the local independent groupwork training agency where the sessions were held. The recruitment literature only suggested that potential group members should be interested in sharing their dreams. We did not interview or select members prior to the start of the first session of each of the three groups. The groups were held in that agency's premises. The room we used was distinctive in that there were no chairs in it but only many large cushions. Group size was between six and twelve. The first group had six members of whom four continued till the end of the third group. The second group contained twelve people, which was really too big, and the third group contained nine members. On average one person started each of the three groups but left after one or two sessions. Members were of all ages, were mainly female, white and professional. Some were married but more often were separated or divorced and with children of varying ages. Several members knew each other previously either through groupwork or circle dancing weekends. Many of the members had interests in what very loosely could be described as New Age pursuits such as yoga, meditation, astrology, circle dancing and aromatherapy. There were two members who attended Quaker meetings and one Methodist member. Otherwise mainstream religious commitments were not evident. Nearly all members presented as heterosexual. Whilst almost all members had been to therapy or personal growth groups before, none had been to dreamwork groups.

Almost all the members who stayed through a group term of ten weeks disclosed either to the group or in the follow-up interviews that they were going through a period of their life which involved, in their eyes, great change or considerable crisis. These crises were typical of the crises of our times, that is, ageing, separation, divorce and work/career stress. Whether the magnitude of these perceived changes differed from the scale of life change normally experienced has not yet been specifically studied. Moreover it became clear that the years following for instance a marriage breakup could still contain a major sequence of 'coming to terms' with the loss and change experienced. Indeed the conscious processing of these 'change' experiences in relation to the recalled dream imagery provided the bulk of the subject matter of the group discussions.

There were two co-leaders, and my colleague was a female freelance groupworker and counsellor. As group leaders or facilitators we prioritised the telling and the working with members' dreams and tended only to disclose our own dreams once each on average during a ten week course. These occasions were when either no member had a dream to present or when, in my case, it was the final week of a group term. There was a level of groupwork expertise and some members were well able to facilitate gestalt and psychodramatic exercises for example. However several members were not so experienced and exhibited reluctance and shyness in relationship to the disclosure of both the detail and form of personal concerns.

Whilst one might expect a high level of cohesion given a relatively sophisticated group membership, this did not preclude significant differences and conflicts emerging at different times. Such differences were, for example, around the centrality of dreamwork in the sessions and related to some members' wish to spend more time on non-dream related personal issues. Another focus of occasional discontent was around the nature of interpretive comment by members, and in particular whether a sexual interpretation of dream imagery was to be prioritised by the group. In the event a core of six group members continued after the finish of the three term programme and have constituted, with the addition of some new members, a self-directed dreamwork group for the last four years.

The group programme usually consisted of a structured round at the beginning in which members shared 'how they were' and gave a short description of any dream they had had and if they wanted to work on it. Then the group would choose two or three dreams to consider during the rest of the evening. The most common method of working with a dream was by suggestion, discussion, association and comparison. The group attempted to help the dreamer to relate their dream imagery to their current daytime, conscious life. We regularly supplemented discussion with action techniques such as the use of gestalt exercises, particularly an emotional identification with different parts of the dream, psychodrama, artwork, meditation and visualisation. The visualisation exercises proved particularly productive and were always based on a powerful image from a member's dreams. Images used in visualisation ranged from 'being a bulb' to 'going on a journey as a bird' to visualising a 'door in the mind' and then going through it. Every session was audio-taped for research purposes and members had access to the tapes. I conducted follow-up interviews with group members a few weeks after the end of the third group. My study of the dreamwork groups was then based upon participation and observation of the groups, supplemented by audio-recording, and subsequent individual interviews with group members.

I will also refer to a more recent team-building and training dreamwork group that I ran for a multi-disciplinary health team. Whenever I quote verbatim from the text of the dreamwork groups I rarely use punctuation so as to try to show the actual flow of the spoken word. I have indicated pauses by the speaker by the use of three dots. I have retained the use of question marks, exclamation marks and quotation marks.

1 The dream in history

The religious dream

Whilst in these dreamwork groups a religious approach was rarely explicitly expressed, historically, a religious perspective on dreaming is highly significant in many of the main world religions. The importance of the dream within both Judaism and Christianity is frequently evident in both the Old and the New Testaments. 'God' is said to communicate with the prophets, such as Abraham, Noah, Daniel, Joseph and Moses through the medium of the dream and likewise 'God' speaks to men and women, such as Mary and Joseph, in the New Testament. Famous dreams from the Bible include Joseph's interpretation of Pharaoh's dream of seven fat and seven thin cows which was interpreted as prohesying seven years of future good harvests to be followed by seven 'lean' years (Genesis, ch.41). Indeed in the Bible dream prophecy can go beyond the interpretation of dreams to include the 'seeing' of the actual dream by the interpretor/seer. Daniel (ch.2) is able both to tell Nebuchadnezzar what his dream has been as well as to interpret it. Such reports of dreams cannot be dismissed since their impact on future society can be very considerable. For example, in Jacob's famous dream at Bethel (Genesis, ch.28) he lies down with his head on a stone. Then, in his dream, he sees Angels going up and down a ladder from heaven to earth and God promises the land upon which Jacob is lying to all his descendants. Contemporary Zionist claims to the ancient kingdoms of Judah and Samaria are in part based upon the Biblical prohecy revealed in such a dream. Indeed a people's dream of homeland, hearth and kin is an essential dynamic in the current conflictual configurations of ethnic conflict in many parts of the world, including Europe. In the popular saying, 'home is where the heart is' we should perhaps rather say 'home is where the dream is'.

Indeed the relationship between reported dream and vision, religious truth and statehood is not confined to the dreams and visions of religious prophets. Parman writes about the importance of a vision and a dream in the conversion of the Emperor Constantine in the early fourth century. As reported, Constantine beheld a vision of a 'flaming cross...in the sky' which was inscribed with the words 'by this sign thou shalt conquer' (1991, p.33). That night, Constantine had a dream in which Christ instructed him to 'adopt the cross as his banner' (Parman, 1991, p.33). Following his victory, Constantine adopted Christianity as the religion of the Western Empire at the Edict of Milan in the following year. Likewise in A.D. 394 Theodosius I, Emperor of Rome, was encouraged at the battle of the river Frigidas by a dream in which the apostle Phillip and John the Baptist appeared. In Islam, as we will see, the dream had a high valuation, whilst in the Hindu tradition dreaming is placed above waking reality in the hierachy of realities (Tedlock 1987a, p.3). Recent religion, such as that of the Baha'i faith, likewise positively evaluates the potential of the dream. The following quotation from the writings of the founder of the Baha'i faith make this clear:

Indeed, O Brother, if we ponder each created thing, we shall witness a myriad perfect wisdoms and learn a myriad new and wondrous truths. One of the created phenomena is the dream. Behold how many secrets are deposited therein, how many wisdoms treasured up, how many worlds concealed. Observe, how thou art asleep in a dwelling, and its doors are barred; on a sudden thou findest thyself in a far-off city, which thou interest without moving thy feet or wearying thy body; without using thine eyes, thou seest; without taxing thine ears, thou hearest; without a tongue, thou speakest. And perchance when ten years are gone, thou wilt witness in the outer world the very things thou hast dreamed tonight.

Now there are many wisdoms to ponder in the dream, which none but the people of this valley can comprehend in their true elements. First, what is this world, where without eye and ear and hand and tongue, a man puts all of these to use? Second, how is it that in the outer world thou seest today the effect of a dream, when thou didst vision it in the world of sleep some ten years past. Consider the difference between these two worlds and the mysteries which they conceal, that thou mayst attain to divine confirmations and heavenly discoveries and enter the regions of holiness (Bahaullah, 1945, pp.32-33).

Indeed, even within a religion, the significance and role of the dream can significantly vary over time as Kruger (1992, pp.57-82) demonstrates throughout his study on the ambivalent position of the dream in early and medieval Christian thought. This ambivalent view of the dream, still evident today in the popular view of dreams, Kruger (1992, pp.19-24) traces back to late-antique authorities such as Macrobius. Macrobius presents five different and hierachically ordered categories of dreams ranging from the true and the revelatory (*oraculum and visio*) to the false and mundane (*visum and insomnium*). Yet mediating this opposition of true and false dreams, Macrobius suggests a middle type of dream (*somnium*) in which truth is represented in fictional, allegorical and metaphorical form (Kruger

1992, p.24). I will show later how the dreamwork groups I studied often came to understand dream imagery as a form of metaphorical truth. Classification of the dream within a religious perspective typically focuses however, not on the discovery of some latent psychological or existential meaning, but rather on reaching a correct perception of the authority and purpose of the dream as meant by the spiritual authority which has invoked the dream. Such a classification involved in medieval Islam, for example, an applied understanding of hierognosis (Corbin 1966, p.384). Hierognosis refers to the hierachical classification of the different orders of visionary knowledge displayed both in dreams and waking realities. Therefore dreams would be interpreted by oneirocritical means by reference to the status of religious imagery appearing in any dream. The dream had a special status in Medieval Islam as the Koran was partly revealed to the Prophet in dreams and the Prophet apparently spoke regularly with his companions about their dreams. Dream interpretation involved particularly the assessment of whether the dream image and its apparent meaning emanated from angels or demons (Meier 1966, p.422); demons being able, in dreams, to manifest themselves as angels. The oneirocritical assessment hinged on the context of the dream and particularly on whether the dream advocated moral or immoral choices, as angels would be unable to advocate 'evil' as the concept of 'evil' was understood in Islam.

Whilst in this section I have focussed on major world religions, the dream has played a significant role in religion in third world societies as for instance Jedrej and Shaw show in their work 'Dreaming, Religion and Society in Africa' (1992). Moreover the contemporary use of dream accounts in evangelical Christian churches in Africa is analysed by Charsley (1992) in the same volume. Here Charsley delineates the role of the dream in the founding of new Christian churches, cultural innovation in religious services and practices, the acquisition of church membership, the contribution of members to the church and to the development of special charismatic powers.

'The imaginal world'

Interestingly, it is in the Sufi tradition within Islam (Corbin 1966, p.406) that the concept of the 'imaginal world' is developed to define a discernible world between that of sensibility and intelligibility. This 'imaginal world' is defined as a world of autonomous forms and images which is apprehended directly by the imaginative consciousness and was held to validate suprasensible perception. This concept of the 'imaginal world' reappears in Jung's (1959, p.49) concept of the 'active imagination', Assagioli's (1965, p.144) theory of psychosynthesis and visualisation techniques, and Rowan's (1993, p.51) presentation of transpersonal psychology. I will later describe, in chapter five, aspects of the use of 'imagework', or 'visualisation' as it is often called, in contemporary psychotherapeutic practices and in the

14

dreamwork groups studied. Suffice it here firstly to recognise the apparent genesis of the concept of the 'imaginal world' in the Islamic theory of the visionary dream; secondly, to recognise that the contemporary anthropology of dreaming is beginning to develop this concept of the 'imaginal world' to critically discern the culturally diverse relationships between the concepts of the dream and waking reality (Tedlock 1987a, pp.3-4). Price-Williams (1987, pp.246-61) subsumes both the capacity to dream and 'actively to imagine' within the concept of the mythopoetic function in humans. The mythopoetic function, a term introduced by Ellenberger (1970, p.314), is essentially a formulation of the creative capacity of the imagination to generate spontaneous imagery which are open to interpretation. The conceptualisation of an 'anthropology of the imagination' is separately taken up in Duerr's 'dreamtime' which argues coherently and philosophically for an integration of imaginative products within the concept of the 'real' (1985, pp.89-103). Price-Williams recommends that the task for anthropology is to elicit why some imaginary products gain social support and others do not. However, such a view denies the possibility of both a partial cultural structuring of the unconscious and a contextual study of the narrative account of the visual imagery.

Culture and the dream

Parman (1991) has recently studied the role of the dream in Western intellectual culture. Taking a broad sweep through the history of Western thought she has plotted both how dream accounts have significantly influenced cultural production as well analysing how the development of dream theory was related to broader epistemological change. As Kruger also expounded, ambivalence, change and fascination are hallmarks historically in the evaluation of the dream. Whereas Aristotle in his *On dreams and On divination in sleep* perceived dreams as by-products of natural and particularly digestive processes (reminiscent of the folk idea of eating cheese last thing at night 'causing' nightmares), St. Augustine saw the dream as an activity of the soul with the potential for contributing a more enlightened perception of reality than was possible through the concrete senses. St. Augustine based his assessment of dream on his distinction between three types and ascending levels of knowledge, that of the body and the senses (*corporale*) that of the imagination (*spiritale*) and that of the intellect (*intellectuale*) (Parman, 1991, pp.49-50). Parman shows for instance how in the Middle Ages in Europe the dream became:

a bridge to ways of knowing, and in the form of the dream vision of the High Middle Ages became a potent symbolic vehicle for expressing medieval ways of knowing (1991, p.50).

She illustrates this, for example, through both Chaucer's and Dante's use of the dream as an allegorical form. The Pilgrim's Progress begins with the dream of Christian and his symbolic journey to Mount Zion. Parman uses the literary notion of allegory as a way to express how historically the dream meaning has been perceived. In a similiar way to my own later use of the concept of metaphor, she sees 'allegory as the veiling of truth in images' (1991, p.50). Allegory, like metaphor, 'is a vitally important form of expressing ideas because that is how humans think--from the concrete to the abstract...' (1991, p.50). Nor do the Middle Ages in Europe see the end of this both positive and ambivalent evaluation of dream. Parman reports how Descartes, the French philosopher particularly renowned for his championing of the rational method, was theoretically inspired by a series of three dreams which imaginatively prefigured the development of his philosophy. His philosophy did however come to negate dream as a source of knowledge (Parman, 1991, pp.83-85).

Religious perspectives and the group case-study

Within the group studied overt religious adherence and belief was only occasionally evident, though a significant minority of group members referred to religious practices, such as church going. I am using the term 'religious' in this setting to define a rare attitude by a group member to perceive the dream primarily as a 'spiritual communication' emanating from a 'divine being'. The consequence of this perspective is that the purpose of 'dreamwork' is confined to hearing, understanding and if necessary obeying the instruction inherent in the dream 'message'. The one dream narrated to the group which was presented as being a 'religious' dream in the sense outlined above was as follows:

Someone was claiming to be my mother but not my mother...and got married to a man with two children...a boy and a girl...the boy was handicapped and totally twisted...his body was all twisted and he couldn't do anything for himself...not only his body that was twisted...he was also a very malicious and a very devilish kind of personality and his sister was about ten or eleven...to look at her was very attractive and she did her brother's bidding and any devilish thing he planned she would put into fulfilment and because I was their sister by their parent's marriage I couldn't get away from them and they made my life hell...I don't know why the girl was healthy and attractive...a normal kind of child...I couldn't go to anyone about my problems...the life I had got with them because the boy created pity and the girl didn't look bad she looked normal...so attractive and if I had told anyone what I was going through...don't know why but the girl was having tubes put into her back...I was told to put the tubes into her and coolly calmly I was going to murder that girl...instead of tubes I got cannulas with rods in the

16

middle...I put cannulas near blood vessels...I was going to release the
cannulas and the girl was going to bleed to death slowly...I wasn't going
to be found out...she was wearing loose blue dresses and so no-one
would notice the blood and so I put the cannulas in and I knew they were
in the right situation and I walked away waiting for the day for me to
release them...before I got the chance to take the rods out the boy and
the girl said to me jointly 'we know what you are doing what you are
planning we have made your life really bad...we would apologise to you
and go away and leave you in peace'...and I woke up.

The narrator of this dream effectively prevented discussion or suggestion from the group as to how she might approach thinking about the dream. She combined a monologue about the 'events' in the dream with considerable self-disclosure. She spoke about the dream in terms of experiencing 'devilishness from the dream'. Later in the individual interview with this dreamer she spoke of the dream being 'a warning' about future events in a particular setting. She referred to dream images as 'having to happen' and the dream as being 'prophetic'. The other members referred subsequently, particularly in the individual interviews, to this dream narration as having been profoundly unsettling. Indeed this was the only occasion in the two hour groups when a break was called for after this dream narration and in the middle of the session. The effect on the dynamic and life of the group of having one member who resisted the ethos of the group and who had a singular view of the meaning of dreams will be presented in chapter six.

Whilst this dream, the only one narrated by this member, was the only evidently 'religious' dream in the sense I have described, reference to imagery from religious texts was occasionally evident in the narration and subsequent discussion. One member dreamt the words, *'the years that the locusts have eaten'* and had been helped to find the rest of the biblical reference, 'I will restore the....' (Joel Ch.2.v.25:748). Later in discussion in the group she felt the reference was meaningful in the context of her present feeling about her coming to terms with the loss of her years in a marriage which was now being dissolved. Here however religious imagery is being used metaphorically.

2 C20 psychological approaches to dreamwork

The Freudian perspective

Freud's pioneering work on the structure of the psyche and the role and function of the unconscious is extremely well known and many of his insights have passed, not always exactly, into the popular culture of understanding dreams. Freud proclaimed the interpretation of dreams to be 'the royal road to a knowledge of the unconscious activities of the mind' (1953,5, p.608) and saw dreams as being the repository of the unfulfilled wishes and desires of the dreamer. In particular Freud (1974, pp.143-156) distinguished between the manifest content of the dream and its latent content. The manifest content was made up of motifs derived usually from the trivialities of daily experience, which he called the day residue. The latent content referred to the hidden, repressed and unconscious meaning of these motifs or images which was buried in a distorted form within the manifest content. The transformation or distortion of the latent content of the unconscious takes place through the processes of dramatisation, symbolisation, condensation, displacement and secondary elaboration (Rivers,1918, p.389). Dreamwork then became for Freudian analysis the bringing to light, through free association, of the repressed aspects of the self. Often these repressed aspects referred to incomplete aspects of childhood development, such as the unfulfilled Oedipal wishes of the dreamer, or to a similar traumatic event. Dreams then are 'the guardians of the sleep' (Freud, 1953, 4, p.233) as dreams allow the safe and hidden expression of repressed wishes. Freud also elaborated the important distinction between primary process and secondary process thinking. Primary process thought is for Kracke, 'a highly condensed, visual, or sensory, metaphorical form of thinking'. Secondary process thinking is defined as conscious, 'centred on language and is linguistically communicable' (1987, p.38). Dreaming is for Freud, par excellence, primary process thought which he regarded as a more primitive form of thinking which also formed the core of myths and fairytales. Such an important distinction has however been challenged and Kracke reviews this debate, concluding that:

> Primary process thought is a qualitatively different kind of thought from secondary process and is just as much subject to maturation and refinement as the latter (1987, p.37-40).

The critique of the hierachical relationship between these two kinds of thought is significant as it opens the way to evaluate dream imagery as an important means for integrating the social, as well as the unconscious experience of the person. The capacity of the unconscious mind to represent unresolved conflict through imaginative processes is central to most psychotherapeutic systems of thought. The generative capacity of the mind to creatively represent conscious and unconscious concerns in dream imagery is crucial to varying forms of dreamwork. What is at issue is what daytime concerns the mental imagery of sleep stands for and how it is generated. Once dream imagery was seen as a potentially decipherable code, the way was open for varying formulations of the meaning of the symbol systems of the sleeping mind. Within the dreamwork groups studied, the Freudian approach was consciously articulated mostly in relation to the popularisation of Freud's view that most symbols, and particularly many common ones, reflected repressed sexual desires (1). There was a view expressed in the group that typically long thin objects would represent the phallus whilst container type objects would represent the vagina and womb. Often there was joking about such perceived representations. Sometimes there was disagreement and interpersonal conflict generated by a member attempting to impose such a sexual interpretation upon a member's dream. The most evident example of this process is discussed in chapter six. Overall the group members brought a Freudian interpretive approach into the discussion on dreams in so far as Freud has laid down certain parameters from which all contemporary psychological perspectives tend to derive. As already indicated, these parameters include his crucial distinction between primary and secondary process thinking, the distinction between manifest and latent meaning and his account of symbolisation. Indeed his evaluation of dreams as potentially meaningful and indeed therapeutic is the foundation for twentieth century dreamwork approaches.

Revised psychoanalytic approaches

Whilst a Freudian perspective is the classical twentieth century perspective on the meaning of dreams, his findings have been substantially developed particularly in what Fosshage describes as a 'revised psychoanalytic model' (1987, p.28). In this revised psychoanalytic perspective the basic distinctions between primary and secondary process thought and between the manifest and latent meanings of the dream have been re-evaluated.

Dreaming in this neo-Freudian perspective is seen rather as a manifest problem-solving and integrative process that takes place as metaphorical thought. Primary process thought is, within this recent model, perceived as being a different but equal form of mentation that is capable of refinement and development during the subject's life. Complex mental operations, such as the solving of mathematical problems, can be achieved in dreams (Fosshage,1987, p.28). Moreover, the adoption of this model allows for a focus on the manifest content of the dream as being of predominant value for interpretation. No longer is the manifest content considered important solely as a device with which to freely associate in analysis. Rather, the metaphorical imagery of the manifest content is the most appropriate available representation of the issue or conflict being expressed in the dream. Fosshage describes this appropriateness as:

Hence, a dreamer usually selects a particular dream figure, not to be a disguised stand-in for someone else, but rather because the figure within the dream context is a most poignant representative of the particular issues at hand (Fosshage,1987, p.31).

The classic perception of the 'real' meaning of the dream being deeply disguised changes then into a focus upon the manifest images and symbols of the dream. Moreover, the dream is seen as being 'prospective', as I aim to show in the next chapter, through Basso's and Jung's view that the dream is future-orientated, rather than orientated to the infantile past. It is also adaptional. Dreaming is then a problem-solving and integrative process occurring as metaphorical thought. Glucksman summarises this revised model as:

Dreaming mentation regulates threatening impulses and feelings by means of its defensive operations, and facilitates the acquisition of new insights, fresh perceptions, and adaptive solutions to current dilemmas in the light of past experience (Glucksman,1987, p.20).

The old adage of 'sleep on it' as a way of resolving conflict and finding new solutions to life's predicaments can be seen as reflecting such a progressive view. No longer does the dream have to be interpreted by the expert analyst but rather is more democratically accessible to thoughtful dreamers. Many of the dreams and the understandings of them reached by group members and presented in this thesis illustrate for the dreamer the potential value of the manifest imagery of the dream. The following dream and its interpretation will suffice to illustrate this point and represent many others, some of which will be presented later in the thesis:

I was in a crowd of people and I was watching some sort of marital official ceremony...and there were some men in formation I think either on parade or dancers wearing very striking clothing for performance or

uniform...the ceremony finished...I was standing back in the crowd and I
couldn't see well...people dispersed a bit...I could see better and there
was a stage and a door at the back opened and a group of people came
out and there was going to be a wedding between a very ugly gross
capitalistic man with a leer on his face and a very young weeping and
despairing young woman...and she went to the extreme left and on right
was the agent who had arranged all this and who was a malevolent
character with wolfish teeth...there were family members there and there
was a clergyman and it was all Dickensian and I woke up before the
marriage and she was standing there sobbing.

The above powerful dream allowed the dreamer to recognise both to
herself and to the group her overall estimation of her own marital situation
and the family reasons for her original marriage decision. The manifest
imagery of the 'unhappy marriage' clearly represented to the dreamer,
though still with significant distortions, her own perception of her marital
situation.

A Jungian perspective

Jung, like Freud, is a twentieth century giant in the field of dream
interpretation. Jung is important for dream interpretation in several ways.
He developed the idea of the collective unconscious, the archetypes and the
theory of the dream as compensatory. As already introduced, his technique
of 'active imagination' is significant as a key technique enabling people to
access less conscious states and fields of imagination. The concept of the
'collective unconscious' was developed by Jung to represent his perception
that the human psyche contained impersonal and archaic contents that
manifested themselves in the myths and dreams of humans. Jung's idea that
all humans contained a common and universal storehouse of psychic
contents is in contradistinction to Freud's view of the unconscious as
consisting primarily of a personal unconscious. Jung defined the difference
thus:

> Whereas the personal unconscious consists for the most part of
> *complexes,* the content of the collective unconscious is made up
> essentially of *archetypes* (italics as in original) (Jung,1959a, p.42).

For Jung the collective unconscious was a pre-given, something inherited
by all people. The Jungian archetypes are the tendencies of the psyche to
manifest patterns and forms in certain particular ways. They are not in
themselves the actual culturally specific representations as perceived in
dream and fantasy, though Jung was not always clear about this distinction
(Samuels,1985, p.33). Archetypes formulated by Jung include the self, the
shadow, the anima and animus, the mother, the child, the wise old man and

the trickster figure. Jung (1951, p.109) maintained that the archetypes can never be fully known. They have a noumenal, awe-inspiring quality and only their manifestation can be observed in an ordered form in myth, and in a more disorganised way in dreams and fantasy. Jung's theory of the archetypes has bewildered many psychologists and certainly empirical definition is difficult. However, taking the example of the anima archetype, Jung (1964:31) broadly defines this archetype as being the 'feminine aspect' of a man. Within this definition the multifarious representations of the the 'female' in the dream may represent positive and negative aspects of this 'feminine self' of the male. For instance a man may contain both representations of the 'muse' as inspiring 'genius', and also that of the siren who lures man to his downfall. Neither image represents the 'anima' in its totality but both are aspects which can be recognised and given meaning through dreamwork. Further, the anima for a man can be the principle of relatedness to the unconscious.

Jung's view of the anima has been critiqued by feminist writers, such as Wehr (1987), as representing a timeless and decontextualised view of the relationship between male and female that is inevitably sexist. Whilst Wehr (1987, p.125) affirms his recognition of the feminine and creative aspect of the self, she advises a definition of the feminine that has emerged from women themselves. Within the dreamwork groups studied there was a definite, albeit popular, awareness of Jung's theory of the archetype and the collective unconscious. Reference was often made to 'this is an archetypal' dream or image in the dream. Welman and Faber (1992, p.65) have distinguished between 'archetypal' and 'personal' dreams through the presence in archetypal dreams of myths and mythological motifs, a strong affective intensity and a feeling of 'remoteness from daily life'. In the groups studied such references were made when the image considered was perceived as being universal in some way. Hence a child motif in the dream of a man in the group was considered archetypal, whereas a series of child images in the dreams of a young women were not. In the former case the interpretation arrived at was that the child image represented the lost intuitive aspects of the person's life as well as the 'mourning' for a lost childhood, whereas in the latter case the dream image was felt to signify an unconscious concern with maternal desire. The group process amplified the various symbols from dreams into a form of 'mini-archetype'. Symbols such as 'bread', 'button' and a 'sherry glass' developed into evocative and contemplative images that were good for the group to think with. As one member said:

Dream images are common to people and common issues come out of collective underlying themes...therefore working on a dream puts you in touch with your own issues...it is neither here nor there who had the dream.

The use of dream symbols, such as the bird, the bulb and the door which were all derived from the dream imagery of the members to focus guided fantasies upon, also had a similar effect of generating these symbols into mini-archetypes or essential metaphors. Reference to mythological stories to help discern possible meaning in dream imagery was evident on occasion. In one instance a woman reported a dream, a part of which referred to a sherry glass being in her hair. In the discussion of this image reference was made to the Samson and Delilah myth, the common symbolic interpretation of the cutting of hair and its equation with the loss of virility. This example, however, shows how the use of such a myth as that of Samson and Delilah can potentially fix female sexual power within an imaginative order that affirms male virility and feminine deceit. Jung's theory of the 'compensatory' function of dreams is well known. Jung saw the role of dreams as:

to restore our psychological balance by producing dream material that re-establishes, in a subtle way, the total psychic equilibrium (Jung, 1964, p.50).

He gives as examples people who are arrogant or ambitious dreaming of flying or falling. He regarded dreams in this sense as warning people about their one-sidedness. Jung is not alone in his 'discovery' of the compensatory theory of dreaming. Holy (1992, p.88) shows how the Berti tribe in Africa, for instance, often considered that the dream image represented its opposite. Therefore to dream of birth was considered as possibly referring to death. Overall the above key ideas of Jung's thinking informed the dream theory of the group in several ways. Members perceived that dreams might involve impersonal and common symbols and that these were not reducible in a Freudian sense to sexual referents. Rather the symbols referred in some rather arcane way to becoming more complete, more oneself. In this sense there was some recognition of what Jung (1959b, p.275) termed the 'individuation process', being the evolving union of conscious and unconscious aspects of a life, working through dream contents and the reflective process the dreamer applied to their own consideration of these symbols. Jung (1964, p.90) saw the dream as a natural and normal phenomenon. It did not mean something other than it was. He quotes the Talmud which says of dreams, 'The dream is its own interpretation' (Jung, 1964, p.90). Jung prefigured the contemporary dreamwork movement's focus on the manifest content of the dream and conceptualised the dream as anticipating possible futures and not as referring back to infantile pasts. For Jung the dream is a symbolic sketch of the future, and a treasure house for self-discovery.

Transpersonal psychology

Transpersonal psychology has already been referred to for its interest in 'imaginal thought' and for its advocacy of visualisation and guided fantasy as key methods in the practice of the therapy. Transpersonal psychology is broadly based on Jungian thought, particularly his theory of archetypes, and on his practice of active imagination as a technique. Assagioli, according to Rowan (1993, p.40), first used the term transpersonal as part of his articulation of psychosynthesis. Assagioli (1967, p.8) distinguished between the more impersonal 'prepersonal' archetypes as defined by Jung, and what he called the 'transpersonal' archetypes of the superconscious. The superconscious is, for Assagioli, the higher creative and intuitive aspect of the self. The aim in transpersonal psychology is to connect the ego with its superconscious, its 'higher self'. This connective process is facilitated through a series of guided fantasy journeys usually in a group setting. A conceptual advantage of the transpersonal perspective on the theory of the archetypes is that many more themes emerging from the imagination can be viewed as archetypal. Instead of the limited number of true Jungian archetypes, any common symbol such as the flower or the journey can be seen in context as archetypal. So the transpersonal theory of archetypes validates such a description of important symbols evoked and developed by the group, such as 'button', 'loaf', 'bulb', 'bird' or 'door'. At least two group members had participated in transpersonal psychology weekends, and on two occasions they reported a development of imagery between the transpersonal psychology experiences and those of their dreams and fantasy journeys in the group. The narration of these fantasies in the dreamwork groups studied often appeared to be describing a sequence of personal mythical events that sometimes related to previous fantasy journeys. The narration of these fantasies was often structured as a dream sequence with a distancing of self involved, and a narration of the apparently bizarre and incomprehensible. The following example is a description of a fantasy journey of a woman in the group. The fantasy was of 'becoming the bird' based on the dream of another group member, described above:

I was on a beech tree...beautiful big tree on a mound with others around...I was a lovely dusky soft brown bird sitting on a nest in a crook of a tree...I was two birds...this brown bird stayed there all the time and I was also a beautiful bird...coral colour...big...strong wings on top of the tree..I took off and a strange thing happened and I was in a great forest and I was looking down on a stone circle and there was a young woman on a flat rock in a white dress as a sacrificial victim and I went down and picked her up in my very strong claws...I went off to a cliff somewhere and put her on a ledge and she went into a cave...I was worried she would get vertigo and fall off the edge...I flew off to a snowy peak...beautiful like a volcanic cone and I am looking down and I go to explore an enormous lake and woodland with creatures...deer...a rabbits and flowers...and I soared up past these cliffs again and I came down to land again...and I was a bit confused as to who I was...I was a hen bird or self/human and I was at a stone circle and there was this lovely women in white again and I assumed she was the same woman again and she was called Daphne and she wanted to give me gave me a beautiful all faceted round crystal in a black cloth...then flew back to the tree...it is quite fascinating.

Clearly the dreamer found this imaginative sequence fascinating and she was able to identify the woman in the fantasy and the stone circle with previous motifs from the fantasy journey made outside the dreamwork group in one of the transpersonal weekend sessions. Mythological features abounded in her description of both fantasy journeys. The motifs of the stone circle, the sacrificial drama, the rescue from the air, the escape to a mountain peak and the crystal gift from the rescuer locate this sequence as in some sense dream-like and therefore involving the same issues and dynamics of narration and communicative context for my analysis. Several motifs that can be considered as transpersonal archetypes or 'mini-archetypes' are contained in both fantasy journeys, such as those of the stone circle, the potential sacrifice, the diamond and the woman, Daphne. In the second example the dream imagery prefigures the motifs of the transpersonal fantasy journey. In the dream, which is long and contains a recognisable sequence and structure, a 'green man' steals a small square box and a large key and throws the key and box onto a ledge so as to hide it. Only one 'brown woman' saw the 'green man' hide the box. The brown woman got the box and the key from the ledge and took them back to her flat. The green man later came back and violently searched all the flats. This is a brief summary of the parts of the dream referring to the key and the box. In the individual interview she talked about how the key and the box had reappeared for her spontaneously in the fantasy journey on the transpersonal weekend only a week later:

I feel the dream is very well explained now...in most areas it makes sense...I had it a week before going on Transpersonal two which was on the male and female principles...on the weekend we were meant to set out to get a chalice and a sword (in the fantasy journey)...*but I came back with a box and a key which had been in the dream...so the dream prefigured the fantasy by a week...I refound the box and the key...I feel they are masculine and female symbols...in the dream the box is locked...I opened it in fantasy ...couldn't open the box in the dream as the key was bigger than the lock...in the fantasy the box has a golden cup in it and I close the box and take it to a wise person and she told me to open it again and it had a silver spear in it which was the moon and I took the moon out of the box and I went down the hill with the moon in my left hand and the key in right hand...amongst the most exciting experiences in my life...haven't put it down since sailing on....*

25

This mythical drama, which the person found most significant at a turning point in her life, contains imagery from her dream of a week before. The image of the key and the box from her dream reappears, apparently in defiance of the group leader's instruction to 'take a chalice and a sword', in the fantasy journey. This reappearance contains a progression however as, whilst in the dream the box cannot be opened because the key is too big, in the fantasy journey the box is opened with important results for the woman. The symbol of the moon represents for the woman the reclamation of part of her feminity, lost for years in an unfulfilled marriage. Both these examples show progression and transformation of symbols between fantasy and dream. Both contain transpersonal archetypes such as the moon, the box, the key, the sacrifice and the diamond. Moreover the pattern of the stories in the reported dreams and fantasies is mythical in so far as the story sequence primarily contains impersonal symbols and themes and is analogous to legend, folklore and fairytale. Moreover the dreamer/fantast's attitude to the imagery defines the symbolic pattern as archetypal in a transpersonal sense. Hillman (1985, p.23-24) views such archetypes as being defined by their 'emotional possessive effect, their bedazzlement of consciousness so that it becomes blind to its own stance' as well as by their content. The theory and practice of transpersonal psychology was then a significant feature and way of approaching, defining and understanding dream and fantasy symbolism in the dream groups.

Gestalt

The gestalt perspective in the group was very important as one member defined herself as a gestalt therapist, and gestalt techniques, which I will expand on in chapter five, were an important technique regularly used in working with the dream imagery. Gestalt therapy was the creation of Fitz Perls (1969). His theory rejected the notion of an unconscious and focused on a concern with the person 'getting in touch with the here and now' and 'being in touch with their feelings'. Dreams in gestalt theory are 'the high road to integration' rather than Freud's 'high road to the unconscious' (Houston,1982, p.44). Each part of the dream is seen as a part of the person that potentially they can get in touch with through dreamwork. Even an insignificant part of a dream is an opportunity to develop a further emotional integration of the various aspects of the self. Perls has written:

> The dream is an existential message. It is more than an unfinished situation; it is more than an unfulfilled wish; it is more than a prophecy. It is a message of yourself to yourself, to whatever part of you is listening. The dream is possibly the most spontaneous expression of the human being, a piece of art that we chisel out of our lives. And every part, every situation in the dream is a creation of the dreamer himself. Of course, some of the pieces come from memory or reality, but the

important question is what makes the dreamer pick out this specific piece? No choice in the dream is coincidental.....every aspect of the dream is a part of the dreamer, but a part that to some extent is disowned and projected onto other objects
(1971, p.27).

Gestalt therapy is an action approach to re-experiencing the self in a more complete sense. Hence in gestalt dreamwork the dreamer is advised to see each part of the dream as a part of themselves. They are asked to identify emotionally with all or part of the dream imagery. Hence they speak of their dream not as about something 'out there' and impersonal but rather they would say, 'I am the ....', speaking always in the present tense. Often the dream narrator uses two chairs or cushions, one to sit in when 'being the dream', and one when they are themselves. Effectively this allows them to dialogue between different aspects of themselves and this can be a powerful and cathartic experience. I will give an example now of a group member doing a gestalt identification with a 'being a sherry glass' which in her dream was a hair roller in her hair! Further examples of the use of this gestalt technique will be given in chapter five on methods of working wirh dream and fantasy imagery.

D. Suggests X. imaginatively identifies with being a wine-glass:
Y.   *Let your hair down!* laughter
X.   *You are very serious about it.*
Others: *We are...we are...we're riveted.*
X1. (X1 = narrator as sherry glass) *I am a wine-glass...slender...old... valued.* (laughs).
F.   *What is it like in X.'s hair*
X1.   *Not the right place...might break...don't want to be in her hair or in her pocket...might get crushed.*
D.   *How do you feel about being old and valued?*
X1.   *I like being valued...not old...vision of being used a long time.*(laughs)...*Oh dear* (X. obviously has an insight into the meaning of what she has said).
X1.   *I feel very squashed in the pockets...want to be seen in a display cupboard.*
I.   *Do you want to be drunk from?*
X1.   *I enjoy being filled up with sherry...it is my use...lovely pale dry sherry.*
D.   *It gives pleasure.*
X1.   *Yes.*
X1.   *It has a lovely effect on the brain...lets everything flow away.*
T.   *Sounds quite aristocratic...fino sherry.*
X1.   *Yes special you see.*
T.   *How do you feel in M.'s hair?*

27

X1. (bit missing) *Bound in straight hair...will make X. look better...a bit demeaning...used in this way...feel unsafe in pocket...squashed...very unsafe in hair.*

D.   What is your relationship with X.

X1.   She values me...um ...out of character in a way.

Y.   Then why in the hair.

X1.   It was the only thing she had to hand to use or...it was convenient...when I feel I am being a sherry glass I feel very good (laughter) *very gracious.*

X.   Not sure which part of me is the sherry glass...I keep wanting to say 'I am very old' (emphasised)*...handed down from grandmother...slender also...I have lasted a long time (emphatically spoken).* End of gestalt exercise.

In the ensuing discussion personal feelings of fragility, age, being valued and long used sprang up on account of this exercise. She immediately related these to her current emotional situation of coping with recent divorce and separation. Issues of power and the use that is made of someone were facilitated through later discussion as were current feelings about herself. Personal meaning of the hair symbol was sought through spontaneous association and insight into metaphorical language use such as the sexualised meaning of 'letting your hair down'. Ideas from gestalt theory and practice figured prominently in group discussion and practice. The gestalt practice of identifying with a significant part of a dream was the most common technique used except for group discussion and suggestion. The idea that the dream imagery referred only to oneself and had no meaningful relationship to external events was an important perspective often voiced in the group. The gestalt perspective is clear that all dreams are to be understood subjectively. There was often ambivalence about external referents to dream imagery. If a female group member dreamt of their male partner, did they perceive the image to be potentially disclosing of an aspect of their partner, an aspect of their 'male' self or to be a metaphorical statement about their relationship to their partner? Whether to understand a dream image in an 'objective' or a 'subjective' way was always a key issue in the group, and also was sometimes a concern between a dream group member and a partner. For instance in a 'jealousy' dream in which the female dreamer dreams about seeing her male partner dancing intimately with another woman at a party, she understood this imagery as being relevant to his possible behaviour. The dreamer had woken up following this dream, feeling that the dream was very real and as a consequence felt quite rejected. She had described this dream to her male partner who advised her to 'interpret' the dream image of him as part of herself! He advised her to explore the part of her that wanted to be at the party and having a good time and not to blame him in reality for her dream imagery of his unfaithfulness. Here the politics and dynamics of interpersonal relationships intersect with plausibly different ways of relating to dream imagery. Such ambivalence about whether to proceed with a literal interpretation of a dream image reflects a more common concern in dream interpretation which is discussed in the ethnographic example of the Berti of Sudan in the next chapter. This chapter has presented core psychological perspectives present both in contemporary dreamwork and evidenced in the groups studied. The next chapter considers the social anthropological perspective on the dream.

Notes

1 At first Freud used the term representation to define the transformation of thought into image. Later he developed his theory of symbolisation, hypothesising a common meaning to certain symbols (Freud,1953, e.g. 5.pp.353-60).

3 The social anthropological perspective

Myth and dream

Anthropologists have historically been more concerned than sociologists with the study of dream as an aspect of the social life of the groups they studied. This probably arises from three intersecting factors. First, many of the societies they studied respected the dream and clearly acted upon the insights apparently gained from them. Secondly, therefore, the study of dream became a part of the holistic analysis that partly defined the enterprise of social anthropology. Thirdly, anthropologists were aware that dream and myth had similar features, both being sequences of vivid images and depending upon inner visualisation for communication and impact' (Kracke, 1947, p.32). Kracke regards myths and dreams as being 'closely related', and refers to Burridge's use of the term 'myth-dream' to describe the situation in societies, such as Rastafarian cults, which do not make a clear separation of the two imaginative forms. Myths have been analysed as if they were the dreams of a culture (Abraham,1979, pp.153-210). Moreover, as myth for Lévi-Strauss (1966, p.17) is a form of bricolage, so the dream for Kracke is a form of bricolage in that the dream gathers:

> from among the day residues ready to hand, and uses them to express metaphorically an emotional conflict, and to work out (or work toward) some resolution of it (1987, p.38).

Kracke (1987, p.33) demonstrates in his analysis of Kagwahiv Indian Amazonian society that the Kagwahiv Indians make a fruitful exchange between the associations and interpretations made from their myths and the way they explain their dream imagery to themselves. However, as well as similarities there are differences also, as whilst 'a dream recounted ends as a narrative, a myth begins as one' (Kracke,1987, p.36).

The development of anthropological studies of dreaming

Anthropologists have therefore constantly been confronted with their subjects' concern and different evaluation of dream contents and alternative conceptions of the distinction between objective and subjective reality. Tylor (1871, p.88) perhaps began the cross-cultural interest in dreaming through his understanding of non-literate people's lack of a hard distinction between reality and illusion (Parsifal-Charles 1986, p.477), and his perception that myth creation, mythogenesis, was a product of dreaming by way of animism. Freud's work in the early twentieth century stimulated the first main phase of anthropological enquiry into dreaming. Seligman (1921,1923,1924) sought to test the Freudian hypothesis that the latent meaning of dreams was universal across cultures (Tedlock, 1987a, p.20). Colonial workers were invited to to provide manifest dream materials which were analysed to discover so-called 'type-dreams'. This analysis was conducted without consideration of their cultural and communicative context.

Later, Lincoln (1935, p.22) in his study of North American Indian dreams developed a distinction between 'individual' and correspondingly unimportant dreams, and 'culture pattern dreams' which were significant for the group and actively pursued. Although Lincoln perhaps is given the credit for the development of a typology of dreaming based on ethnographic research (Parsifal-Charles,1986, p.291), even his results are now considered ethnocentric (Tedlock,1987a, p.21). The 1940s and 1950s saw the development of the content theory of dream analysis (Hall, 1951, pp.60-3; Eggan, 1952, pp.469-485; Hall and Van de Castle, 1966, p.17). This attempt to quantify and consequently to analyse cross-culturally partly reflected the culture and personality school of social anthropology. The culture and personality school of North American anthropology sought to identify and analyse core personality traits as being formed by cultural influences. This has continued into the 1980s with the work of Gregor (1981, p.353). Indeed the content analysis of dreams is still used in psychological research. Catalano (1987), for example, recently sought to prove through content analysis that the dreams of emotionally disturbed adolescents are different from those of normal adolescents.

The voluminous extraction of dream symbolism by these anthropologists allowed the compilation of numerous manifest dream reports and their cross-cultural analysis for personality and cultural variables. Whilst this approach does attempt to value the dream positively as psychodynamically and culturally significant, it is, in fact, an approach that decontextualises dreams. The importance of dream narration, dream discourse and indigenous dream theory is almost entirely ignored. Moreover, Crapananzo (1981, pp.145-158) has argued that the ethnocentricism of the content analysis school of dream analysis is based on an epistemology that reduces language to a merely referential function.

The development of ethnopsychiatry from the 1950s onward by Devereux (1980) is another anthropological landmark in the analysis of dreaming. Devereux (1969, pp.139-168) in his work with North American Indian groups sought to further integrate a Freudian approach into anthropological fieldwork. Devereux (1966, p.213) applied Freudian concepts of transference and reality-testing to dream reports as well as making a critical analysis of the concept of pathogenic dream. He was concerned particularly with the notion of causality that underpins this concept. In a study of a Crow Indian Devereux (1969, p.139) analysed his Indian patient's dream within the cultural context of the Crow Indian vision quest and showed how he himself used this cultural context for therapeutic work with this patient. Devereux's work effectively initiated the subject of ethnopsychiatry or transcultural psychiatry. For instance Devereux was able to use in therapy his Crow Indian patient's cultural belief that success in the dream world anticipated successful behaviour in waking reality. Devereux (1969, p.165) showed how the Crow Indian incorporated Devereux as therapist within the identity of a Crow Indian Spirit Being. Devereux facilitated the patient's orientation to reality through the therapeutic use of the patient's culturally sanctioned and prolific dreaming. However, as Obeyesekere (1990, p.21) has pointed out in his criticism of Devereux's culturally specific reflexivity, for Devereux the 'manipulation of ethnic symbols' may only provide adjustment but not introspective self-awareness or 'curative insight'.

Another psychoanalytically orientated anthropological approach to the analysis of dreams was that of D'Andrade (1961, pp.327-8) who analysed the function of dreams in sixty-three societies, using material from the Human Relations Area Files. D'Andrade concluded that dream usage arose out of anxiety, and that in hunter-gatherer societies, where there was a need for more self-reliance than in pastoral-agrarian societies there was also significantly increased use of dreams. By the 1970s dreamwork was beginning to be considered within the context of the cultural system of which it was a part. Crapanzano (1975, pp.145-158) analysed the metaphorical usage of saints and jnuns in the dreamworld of the Moroccan Hamadsha. He showed that personal use of particular dream symbols, and their performative function in terms of conflict recognition and possible solution, were firmly embedded within the 'implicit folk psychology' of the culture.

I have already noted that the similarity between myth and dream is an abiding theme in social anthropology. Kuper (1979, pp.645-662) and Kuper and Stone (1982, pp.1225-1234) attempted to apply the structuralist method of analysis of myth, developed by Lévi-Strauss (1963, pp.206-231), to dream. Kuper considered that the similarity between myth and dream was that both are attempts to cope with problems of reality. These authors proceed to analyse certain dreams and dream sequences as if they constituted a systematic argument which used an ordered set of transformations to reach a resolution. In their analysis they attempt to show

32

that the binary rules that structure mythical thought can be transposed to our understanding of dream content. Whether a structuralist approach of this kind marks a major breakthrough in the understanding of the dream in society is unclear. Tedlock recognised that Kuper had succeeded in discovering 'underlying linguistically coded analytical rules' (1987a, p.27) within the dream narrative. However she and others have raised various criticisms of this approach. The observance of rules does not imply that such rules generate the dream material. Kracke (1987, pp.50-52) as we have seen, argues that myth and dreams are also essentially different in that myths move from verbal narration to sensory imagery whilst dreams move from imagery to narration. Hence the narrative texts of dreams and myths, whilst related as we have already seen, are still dissimilar.

Mannheim (1987, p.151) also implicitly criticises a structuralist analysis of dreaming by his rejection of the idea that structural laws can be discovered in the 'narrative structure of dreams'. Rather he asserts that structural laws exist at the interface between culturally and historically specific interpretive and significatory systems. His view is based on his comparative study of the development, over a three hundred year period, of Andean Indian systems of dream interpretation and myth. Mannheim found that, whereas their understandings of myth had hardly changed, those of dream interpretation had been almost completely transformed. Mannheim (1987, p.149) explained that there was 'a fundamental difference between the way signs function in Andean dreams on the one hand, and in Andean ritual and myth on the other'. This difference arrives because:

Quechua dream interpretations encode only the semantic dimension of language and thus have meaning only in terms of the immediate relationship between signifier and interpretant, while myths encode both the semantic and syntactic dimensions (Tedlock,1987a, p.28).

A structuralist approach, which is concerned with the analysis of the 'latent' analytical binary structure of the dream, can then be a part only of the cultural understanding of dream material, particularly as it is not concerned with the importance of the communicative context of the dream report itself. I do however use the method of binary analysis in chapter five.

A communicative theory of meaning

Anthropologists have continued to develop the concept of the dream report. Tedlock suggested that the manifest dream content:

should be expanded to include more than the dream report. Ideally it should include dream theory or theories and ways of sharing, including the relevant discourse frames, and the cultural code for dream interpretation (1987a, p.25).

Tedlock describes this perspective as a communicative theory of dreaming. This theory has to consider the dream narration as a communicative event involving three overlapping aspects: the act and creation of narration, the psychodynamics of narration, and the culturally bounded group (emic) interpretive framework. Such a theory considers the analysis of dream as more than that of an hermeneutically based text. It is also a social and cultural process or activity with expressive and instrumental outcomes. When this takes place then, we may take seriously Herdt's proposition:

that culture may actually change experience inside of dreams, or that the productions of dreaming do actually become absorbed and transfomed into culture (1987, p.82).

The communicative theory of dreaming then, alerts us to the importance of the psychodynamics of the social setting and the interpretive framework of the participants. The social anthropologist is concerned with the analysis of an interpretive framework which necessarily structures both narration and interpretation. Two examples from Tedlock's edited volume (1987a) illustrate this important point. Basso (1987, pp.86-88) relates her analysis of the dream theory of the Kalapalo Indians of Central Brazil to the differences between Freudian and Jungian perspectives on dreaming. Freud usually related dream imagery to the past whereas Jung saw such imagery as possible symbolic sketches of the dreamer's future. Jung (1948, pp.255-263) called this a *prospective* function of dreams, not to be confused with a *prophetic* function. Jung wrote:

(Dreaming) is an anticipation in the unconscious of future conscious achievements, something like a preliminary exercise or sketch, or a plan roughed out in advance. Its symbolic content sometimes outlines the solution of a conflict (1948, p.255).

Obeyesekere (1990, pp.17&57) also sees a 'progressive' role to dream imagery in that such imagery develops a 'symbolic remove' from the deep motivation that occasions it. Basso saw a progressive theory of dreaming as being those culturally bounded group theories of dreaming that held that dream imagery is future oriented in so far as the dreamer uses dream imagery and its symbolisation of current concerns to speculate upon, and orientate to, future goals of the self. Basso justifies this assertion by claiming:

Dreaming is also a performative event because it causes the future by revealing the dreamer's life as it is encapsulated in current aspirations, moods and inchoately understood motivations and fears of an individual.

34

The dreaming is thus less a matter about what will happen to a person than about the self becoming (1987, p.101).

Also in this volume, Tedlock (1987b, pp.105-129) compared the different ways of dream sharing and dream interpretation between a Mexican and a Guatemalan group, the Zuni and the Quiche, to show how such differences are rooted in contrasting metaphysical and psychological systems. How the living and the deceased are differentially conceptualised is crucial to her analysis. This leads to wholly different interpretive results of similar imagery.

The Tedlock (1987) volume seeks to redefine the boundary between the psychology and the social anthropology of dreaming. The customary distinction between psychology's field being the intra-personal and anthropology's being the social is broken down. Psychology needs to understand how the dreamer uses concepts and language which are, of necessity, culturally based to narrate dreams. Anthropology, on the other hand, has to recognise that the communication and framing of dream narratives are always dependent upon the dream theory of the culturally bounded group.

This development mirrors a more general fusion of self and society which has also been developed within contemporary feminist psychoanalysis (Eichenbaum & Orbach,1982, p.12). Tedlock and her colleagues (1987) then provide an invaluable account of the state of contemporary anthropological analysis as well as offering some key directions for future work on dreams. Although the book, 'Dreaming: Anthropological and Psychological Interpretations', was, in general, well received (Parsifal-Charles, 1986, p.460; Hodes, 1989, pp.6-8), it has been criticised by Hodes (1989, pp.6-8) for its dated view of psychoanalytic thinking. He suggests that psychoanalysis has moved on from its original central concern with relating mental contents, including dream imagery, to a concern with early socialisation. Psychoanalysis now tends to centre on the transference relationship as it is experienced in the here and now by therapist and client. Hodes considers that there is a striking convergence between psychoanalysis and social anthropology and that both are becoming increasingly concerned with the communicative context of dream sharing. The dream in the psychoanalytic group is now seen as contributing to group culture and as being expressive for the group, as well as being indicative of personal transference (Yalom,1985, p.429; Cividini-Stranic, 1986, p.147). Yalom (1985, p.430) uses the example of a dream by a group member about to undress in a room. This was considered by the therapist as expressing the dreamer's mode of silence and their fear of disclosing a personal relationship to the group.

An ethnographic example: the Berti

I have chosen the Berti of the Sudan as a case-study, not because they are in some sense a typical third world bounded group, but because the analysis by Holy (1992) provides a particularly fine example of how an anthropological analysis can illuminate native dream theory. The reader who wishes to study a variety of third world bounded groups is advised to consult the Tedlock volume (1987) or the more recent Jedrej and Shaw (1992) study of dreamwork in recent and contemporary African societies. Whilst Holy does not suggest that the Berti are a typical African tribal society and they are not prolific in either remembering or interpreting dreams, they can represent the widespread human practice of perceiving the dream as meaningful. Moreover this meaningfulness is perceived not in relation to the 'inner mind' but rather the dream is seen as predicting the future in some way that can be considered and worked out through dream interpretation (Holy, 1992, p.86).

In this way Holy writes that the Berti when interpreting dreams are not conducting 'psychoanalysis but semiotics' (1992, p.86). That is they are interpreting signs and they are making connections from one domain, that of the narrated dream image, into another, that of the predicted future. This rule-governed, i.e. semiotic, translation of the encoded message in the dream follows rules which are implicit and are not 'owned' by specialised dream interpretors but are implictly used generally by the Berti to understand their dreams. Firstly the Berti dream interpreter makes a decision whether to interpret the dream literally or analogically. A literal interpretation would envisage a dream of rain, for example, as directly predicting rain. An analogical interpretation would involve seeing the dream image as a metaphor standing for something else. Therefore rain might represent good fortune for instance. Such an initial classification of dream imagery Holy advises is common in disparate societies (1992, p.8). An analogical rather than a literal interpretation is more common amongst the Berti. The decision as to whether to proceed literally or analogically is made by the Berti through a consideration of traditional wisdom about particular dream images. Holy (1992, p.89) gives as an example, in contrast to the rain dream image above, the way an old man interpreted a dream in which he experienced a strong wind whilst sitting under a tree. In this case the old man drew on the collective wisdom that dreaming of wind would refer to something unpleasant occurring. Such a view was 'confirmed' in this instance when the next day there was a savannah grass fire. The Berti, having decided whether to proceed literally or analogically with reference to whether particular signs, such as wind, are present, then ask three basic questions:

1. Should the meaning of the dream be understood as the reversal of its manifest content or not?

2. Does the dream predict some specific event or is its message merely of general significance?

3. Should the dream be interpreted intratextually (by focusing on the dream imagery alone) or should contextual factors (from outside the dream imagery, such as the dreamer's circumstances) be taken into consideration in the proper understanding of its message? (Holy, 1992, p.89).

Holy proceeds to elaborate the complex system of grammar through which the Berti then 'read' the dream for either specific or general reference and meaning. The value of his example, apart from its analytic sharpness, lies in its elucidation of the largely implicit systematic process through which a Berti dream interpretor goes through when interpreting a dream. This rule-bound process is intimately linked to how symbols operate generally in Berti society as in the 'rain' example above. The interpretation of the dream is then necessarily linked to the wider system of cultural meanings through which daily life is experienced by the Berti. I later intend to show how the dream groups I studied similarily used common cultural meanings, embedded in daily language use, to explain their dream imagery.

The Senoi example

The eighties have also seen the probable final collapse of the 'Senoi' theory and practice of dreaming. Stewart (1951, pp.21-33), and later Garfield (1975, pp.80-117) popularised the supposed dream usage of this tribal group in central Malaysia. The debate about the authenticity of their reports, based partly upon the work of anthropologists who studied the Senoi at an earlier date, has rivalled the debate over the authenticity of the Castaneda journals in its public impact (Castaneda et al,1970; Douglas, 1975, pp.193-200). Stewart, on a brief fieldwork base, claimed that the Senoi were a uniquely peaceful and harmonious tribal group, without mental health problems. The cause of this happy state lay in their attitude to, and use of, dreams. Apparently each day the Senoi would hold 'dream workshops' and would work collectively through interpersonal difficulties on the basis of interpreting their imagery. They acted upon their interpretations to avoid future conflicts. Senoi children were, he claimed, taught how to 'incubate' dreams and thus to control their dream life. Stewart's theories on Senoi dreamwork had a major impact on the developing dreamwork movement, particularly in the United States during the last fifteen years, and recently in Europe as well. Most popular dreamwork manuals are significantly influenced by this version of Senoi dreamwork (e.g. Williams, 1984, p.301; Shohet, 1985, pp.78-81). However Domhoff (1985, p.34) demolishes Stewart's claim for a unique Senoi dreamwork culture. Domhoff shows that the Senoi do not have dream workshops and have no unusual dream usage.

Domhoff develops an effective sociological analysis of the 'sixties' human growth movement in the United States and the way in which it adopted Stewart's 'findings' to counter disillusion with contemporary cultural reality.

Ethnography and the dream

Finally, another development of this decade has been the use of both researchers' and informants' dreams for ethnographic research purposes. Dreams are seen as throwing light on the subjective orientation and cultural position of the anthropologist, as well as on the intersubjective encounter between anthropologist and informant. As Hastrup (1992, p.119) has written 'all ethnographers are positioned subjects and grasp certain phenomena better than others'. I think that a reflexive anthropology may in time recognise dream imagery as a valuable source of critical insight into the progress of fieldwork. Levine (1981, pps.276-93) analysed the dreams of three of her informants for transference material concerning her own relationship with these informants. She was able to gain an increased awareness of issues such as power, asymmetry between herself and informants, poverty and dependence and the degree of gender support she was offering to one informant during her marital difficulties. I have tried (Edgar,1989) to relate my dreams experienced during fieldwork to both the stages of fieldwork research and to the eventual analytic themes that developed in my Master's thesis (1986). Whether the anthropological study of the 'other' will necessarily one day embrace the researcher's own unconscious has yet to be seen, although Caplan has suggested, in her discussion of 'engendering knowledge' that:

> ...the time has come for us all, male and female, to recognise that the sense of self which has sustained the practice of ethnography for so long is irrelevant and that as the French poet Rimbaud put it 'Je est un autre' (1988, p.17).

I have here considered briefly the history of social anthropological approaches to dreaming and indicated my conviction that the perspectives developed in Tedlock's edited set of papers offer important ways forward which I have followed in my analysis of the studied groups' dreamwork practice. A communicative theory of dreaming offers, as she suggests, an opportunity to integrate psychodynamic perspectives with 'natural-language, socio-linguistic, semiotic, and interpretive approaches to the study of meaning in others' (1987a:30).

Finally Levine (1991) has explored the role of culture in the representation of conflict in the children of different cultural groups. She compared the reported dreams of Bedouin, Irish and Israeli children along the four dimensions of: a) self-representation in the dream, referring to the activity and involvement of the self in the dream, b) representation of the other dream characters, c) the realistic quality of the dream, and d) the content of the conflict. Levine's findings suggest that content variability, in this case with respect to conflict, is culturally constructed. She related differential patterns of representation in dream imagery to different socialisation processes. For instance she showed that Bedouin children were more likely to have non-human representation in dreams and linked this to greater family and group solidarity. Such family and group solidarity meant that conflict became more threatening and was then outer-focussed by the dreamers. Likewise Irish children were found to have, 'decreased intimacy' between themselves and other dream characters (1991, p.487). She suggests that their dream imagery is reflective of a less emotionally expressive socialisation process. However Kibbutz children were likely to dream directly of conflict and of humans as allies and enemies. Levine links this finding to the difference in parenting and parenting-child relationship patterns within the Israeli Kibbutz system.

Her very interesting results, which I have only briefly indicated, suggest that childrens' ego coping strategies are culturally based and consistently reflected in differential dream imagery patterning. Her results open the door to further studies of patterning and the identification of links between dream imagery and cultural norms. Overall, this consideration of the history of anthropological interest in dreaming as a potentially valuable facet of a society's social life demonstrates the validity of conceptualising dream as a significant field for social anthropologists (and sociologists) to consider. Moreover since doing anthropology at home is now well accepted within the discipline it is appropriate to assert the value of considering the analysis of dream, and dream narration, as a valuable part of the social anthropological enterprise.

The anthropological contribution to dreamwork

The relevance of an anthropological approach to dreamwork can be perceived as follows. Tedlock's communicative theory of dreaming offers an approach that does not abstract the dream and its potential meaning from the social and cultural context in which it is reported. The cultural dynamics of the communication of the dream are part of the process that can be analysed. The relationships that exist within the interpersonal and group context influence the dream report and its negotiated meaning. The theoretical approaches, often latent and implicit, that govern the social construction of possible meaning from the dream narratives can be, if not the object of study, then at least perceived as crucial to the interpretive outcome. Moreover this understanding of the cultural relativity of 'native' theory or theoretical approaches to dream understanding will illumine for the dreamworker the importance of seeing the dream and the dream account within the cultural context of the sub-group with which they are working.

Whilst the idea that the dream image and its potential sense lies within the cultural context of the dreamer may appear obvious, the actual implications of taking this approach are significant. Particularly, such an approach relegates the dreamworker's use of standard guides and dictionaries of symbol interpretation to the past as these standardised approaches prove irrelevant, as we will see later in the ethnography, to working with the actual process of meaning construction within a particular interpersonal situation. Whilst such dream dictionaries may be of interest as background information and as a way of studying a society's particular evalaution of symbols, they do not significantly advance our appreciation of the actual group and culture based construction of meaning from dream accounts. Moreover social anthropology has provided us with a wide array of dreamwork uses in different, largely third-world, societies which make a powerful contribution to a broadening of our awareness of the potential social use of dream imagery. As the Senoi example above shows, sometimes such examples are problematically constructed and can generate a life of their own. Social anthropology has a particular focus on the study, over time, of small-scale culturally bounded groups. This focus is holistic and seeks to understand the complexity of human behaviour through an analysis of the process and fusion of human creativity within the context of larger scale social forces. My study of dreamwork uses such an approach and shows how the human capacity for meaning-making is embedded within the cultural context.

4 Dreamwork and the caring professions

We have already seen in chapter two the ambivalence with which the dream has been regarded in Western history. This may explain the current ignorance about dreamwork in the caring professions, and its lack of presence in for instance the nursing curriculum (Jane and Cooper, 1987). As I outlined in the first chapter, dreams are either seen as the preserve of the psychoanalyst and need an expensive and recondite apprenticeship to decipher their symbolic code, or alternatively are just 'nonsense', perhaps the random outcomes of the banking down of the mind's computers at night. Such an approach misses a lot. Dreams and dreamwork provide an accessible avenue to the 'undefended self'. Dreams and nightmares provide an unguarded approach to the inner conscious and unconscious preoccupations of the self and the anticipations of the future self. Jung (1948a, p.263) wrote of dreams as providing a 'spontaneous self-portrayal, in symbolic form, of the actual situation in the unconscious'. As such they provide key data for the counsellor, therapist, social worker, nurse etc. to work with. This book aims to both inform and equip caring professionals to be able to begin to work with dream imagery, to be able to respond effectively to a service user or patient telling them a dream.

This chapter intends to present an analysis of the use of dreams in welfare practice and medical (non-psychiatric) situations. I intend to show the key themes involved in dreamwork as well as providing a literature search to some of the current areas of non-psychiatric work with dreams. This chapter and the following one on 'methods' of working with dream imagery should provide the basis for a caring professional to begin to work with a dream image. The chapter will also show that dreams, as well as providing evidence of individual's states of mind, can also be used to provide information about how people in certain situations, such as bereavement, cope with transition and loss. The psychological processes underlying the meaning of the term 'coming to terms with ...' are opened up for a more direct examination. Such insights also provide a strong case for further research into the patterning of dream imagery in specific groups of service users.

Grief, loss and transition

In many areas of applied welfare practice, such as in family therapy (Buckholz, 1990) and groupwork (Barrineau, 1992), dreams are being used by practitioners. However it is, perhaps not surprisingly, the case that dreamwork has been most carefully considered in relation to work with the terminally ill and the bereaved. Welman and Faber (1992, p.63) used a Jungian approach to link the creativity of dream imagery to the 'unconscious processes intrinsic to terminal illness'. They aimed to show that dreams actually prepare people for death and dying. Dreams, they assert, do this by helping the individual to consciously orientate to the collective symbols produced by the unconscious in response to their actual situation. In their article they reported a sequence of seven dreams recorded by a terminally ill seventy year old man. This man had no particular interest in dreams or psychology and was resisting the prognosis that he was terminally ill. The dream imagery reported included the 'separation of the body into two parts', being called, 'from the other side by friends', 'driving towards a light at the end of a very long tunnel', 'dancing with two very young and beautiful girls' and finally dreaming of a 'bright flower' that he had always wanted in his garden.

Whilst the Jungian analysis of these symbols in the article richly draws upon mythological sources to attempt to explain the universal meaning of the young girls dancing and the 'bright flower' of the dreams, the other symbols referred to here are more easily understood as possibly being related to dying. For instance the long dark tunnel leading to a bright light is now commonly referred to when discussing the near death experience. Similarily the evocative meaning of 'being called' from the 'other side' by friends is a very literal symbolisation of the dreamer's state. The authors assert that merely by remembering and being exposed to these dreams, the images had a therapeutic effect on the dreamer. They suggest that 'an enlightenment of his conscious attitude followed' (1992, p.70) through his becoming orientated to the numinous power of the dreamt symbol. From this example the authors assert particular features to such dreaming. First they argue that dream imagery can be anticipatory; second, it is progressive; third, that there is a repeated reference to 'post-mortal psychical existence'; and finally, there is a 'concomitant transformation of the personality' (1992, p.77). These important claims assert a value and a meaning to dream imagery that is beneficial to the dreamer even without an analysis of the imagery. The old adage of 'sleep on it' when faced with an insurmountable problem remains then still pertinent!

Even in other content analyses of the dreams of the dying (Prince and Hoffman, 1991) which have not taken such a Jungian stance and which have not evidenced the dying as having archetypal dream imagery they concluded, with Weisman, that:

> dreams continued to function as metaphors in which problems and solutions are conveyed to consciousness (Prince & Hoffman 1991, p.185 quoting Weisman 1972, p.185).

If such progressive, anticipatory and therapeutic outcomes are possibly available from our dream imagery, it is important that such hypotheses are further researched and that professional therapists and welfare workers become acquainted and familiar with how to deal with such imagery. The theme of progression in dreams comes out in another recent article that studied dying, mourning and loss symbolism in the dreams of young adult students. 149 college students were asked to keep dream diaries (Barrett, 1992, pp.99-100) and 1412 dreams were examined for imagery of any deceased person. Furthermore 96 college students, some of whom had experienced a recent bereavement, were asked specifally about any dreams of dead people that they had experienced. A fourfold catagorization of dreams was developed by the author. Dreams of the deceased were typically about 'coming back to life' in which the dead wanted to 'discuss the situation surrounding their death' (Barrett, 1992, p.100); 'advice dreams' in which the deceased proffered advice to the dreamer; 'leave-taking dreams' which were usually experienced as being very positive and beneficial for the dreamer; and finally 'state of death' dreams wherein the deceased, usually by telephone, described, often incompletely, the state of death.

Barrett develops this typology of dreams about the deceased as reflecting the stages of the bereavement process (Kubler-Ross 1969). For instance the 'back to life' dreams relate to the first 'denial' stage of grieving in which fantasies of the return of the loved one are common, whilst the 'leave-taking' category of dreams relates especially to the acceptance stage of mourning. 'Leave-taking' dreams often involved the completion of unfinished business between the deceased and the dreamer. Dreaming then is hypothesised as being a key feature of the grieving process in which the 'incorporation' of the deceased is a vital point in reaching a successful resolution of the mourning process (1992, p.107). So far the material I have been presenting in this chapter about the dream aspect of the grieving process has been describing the dream as something 'given' to the dreamer and the client or patient appears passive in relation to the receipt of their night imagery.

Mogenson (1990) however advocates an imaginal approach to mourning. I have already in chapter one outlined the ancient idea of imaginal thinking and its incorporation in contemporary transpersonal psychology and psychosynthesis. Jung's advocacy of active imagination is also central to this concept and practice. Mogenson, like Welman and Faber, advocates the activation and generation of the images of the unconscious into the conscious mind of the mourner. Particularly useful are the spontaneous images produced by our dreams, but the products of spontaneous or therapeutically assisted reverie are also potentially valuable to the reflective process. Mogenson advocates then an 'elegiac mourning' consisting of an active dialogue with our own bidden and unbidden images of the deceased. Gestalt and psychodramatic procedures are advocated to further generate and facilitate this process, and are described separately in the next chapter. Part of the resolution of the mourning process lies in the discovery of images by the mourner which 'immortalise the dead' (1990, p.325). The imaginative work of the mourning and how it can be assisted by counsellor, therapist or welfare worker is the crucial focus of an imaginal therapy. Mogenson, like Jung also, refers to the Tibetan Book of the Dead (1957) as being a unique example of a definitive crystallisation of the imaginal journey of the deceased through the various Bardo planes leading to rebirth. Whilst the Tibetan Buddhist has such a collective resource through which to understand and even experience the impersonal journey of the loved one, such a resource is largely unavailable to the post-modern Western individual psyche. Hence the derivation of meaning from dreams and other products of imaginal thought have to be sifted in a much more eclectic way for possible transpersonal or archetypal meaning.

A further example of a more active and therapist assisted approach to the imagery of the deceased is described in Malon's case-study (1989). In this example a social worker reflects on how they worked with a young woman's recurrent nightmare of seeing the skeleton of her dead mother. Despite extensive resistance the young woman was strongly advised to turn and face the frightening image of her mother in the dream. After some time the woman did report that she had spontaneously turned and faced the mother image in a dream and could describe what she had looked like and her familiar wedding rings. Following this breakthrough the nightmares appeared to stop. This therapist, like Mogenson, sees dreams as a process to be imaginally engaged with rather than reductively interpreted as in a more Freudian approach.

Finally Golden and Hill (1991) report how they used dream imagery as a way to help patients creatively grieve the loss of the good parents that they had never in actuality experienced. The patient is offered the opportunity to 'reimagine' themselves within the safe space of therapy. The authors suggest that the:

..capacity for reverie, the ability to play, to imagine and to dream - using whatever signifiers are at hand - shifts the balance from the hopelessness of melancholia to the creative work of mourning (Golden & Hill,1991 p.30).

The grieving process comes to completion with the creation of a definite image of the deceased in which the essence of the person is distilled. The authors refer to such an image as a 'psychic keepsake'. Jung's portrayal of the appearance of his dead wife in a dream is a fine example of such a psychic event:

After the death of my wife I saw her in a dream which was like a vision. She stood at some distance from me, looking at me squarely. She was in her prime, perhaps about thirty, and wearing the dress which had been made for her many years before. It was perhaps the most beautiful thing she had ever worn. Her expression was neither joyful nor sad, but, rather objectively wise and understanding, without the slightest emotional reaction, as though she was beyond the mist of affects. I knew it was not she, but a portrait she had made or commissioned for me. It contained the beginning of our relationship, the events of thirty-five years of marriage, and the end of life also. Face to face with such a wholeness one remains speechless, for it can scarcely be comprehended (Jung 1963, p.296).

The mourning process and the imaginative contemplation of their future by the terminally ill has provided therapists interested in dreamwork and imaginal thought with a particularly well suited field in which to study the possible use and meaning of dream and imagework.

Dreamwork and people with learning difficulties

Wunder (1993, p.117-127) reports her research as a sociologist into the day and night (dream) imagery of the siblings of disabled children. She presented her unexpected finding that the respondents' imagery showed a series of common themes in relation to their disabled siblings. These themes included desires and aspirations to be 'a saviour'; guilt that 'they' were normal; the 'notion that someone or something (a fairy Godmother) would change things'; and sorrow about the disability. The author concludes that such day and night imagery represents a potential source of data that researchers could access and use to increase empathy, and knowledge about the key preoccupations, conscious and unconscious of their informants. The author considers that groups such as persons with AIDS, children of alcoholics or people with chronic or terminal illness would benefit from such consideration. Indeed to my mind if the proposition holds that such imaginative data is relevant and valuable to the researcher, the methodology should be usable with any comparable social group. Wunder's article shows that both day imagery and night/dream imagery offer the opportunity to explore profoundly and to understand more deeply core personal, group and social issues.

Work with refugees and post-traumatic stress disorder

The work of Wunder above shows us the potential benefit to be gained by the analysis of the dream life of particular groups of clients, patients and service users. The dream life of refugees is one such therapeutic domain that has been extensively studied by Cernovsky (1988,1990a 1990b). Cernovsky in his study of groups of Czech refugees tried to link the degree of trauma experienced by the refugee in their escape with subsequent sleep disturbance and problems in assimilation to their new country. However among his several findings he was not not able to show such a correlation. However he did show correlations between current sleep disorder and assimilation problems and between current nightmares and difficulty in escaping (1990a). In another paper he shows a negative correlation between the key features of nightmares, such as anxiety or escaping, and the demographic characteristics of the refugees, such as their age and gender (1990b). Cernovsky (1988) also links his findings to more general studies of post-traumatic stress disorder in his thesis that the experience of escaping and becoming a refugee leads to refugees becoming more nightmare-prone. Cernovsky links his findings to those of Hartman.

Hartman (1984) showed that normally recurrent nightmare sufferers have more permeable mental boundaries betwixt fantasy and reality, and between their image of self and others for example. Cernovsky proposed that refugees became more nightmare-prone as their behavoural and cognitive boundaries had to become more permeable to help them cope with adjustment to new language and customs. The prevalence of nightmares has been linked to recent unpleasant life-events.

Cook, Caplan and Wolowitz (1990) studied the dreams of 422 men and attempted to link the prevalence and type of social stressor with the frequency and content of nightmares and dreams. They found that whilst nightmares were linked to classic stressors such as combat exposure, dreams appeared not to be. They found some evidence that nightmares and dreams were a way to work through negative life experience such as combat service in Vietnam. Whilst these studies are exploratory they do alert the caring professional to the potential role and significance of dream and nightmare as a key indicator of exposure to post-traumatic stress disorder. Cushway and Sewell (1992) provide a useful assessment of the role of post-traumatic stress disorder and dreaming, as well as providing direct guidance for counsellors working with this condition. The other studies reported in this chapter claim that the manifest content of the dream is potentially relevant to the client's processing of unpleasant life experience, problem-solving processes and adjustment to changing personal and social life circumstances.

Dreamwork and therapeutic methods

This chapter has so far considered some of the possible therapeutic fields and client groups within which dreamwork has been used for intervention and/or study. Now I intend to continue this study of the presently available literature with respect to the following methods of intervention: counselling, groupwork and family therapy. Recently the counselling field has produced relevant books on using dream and imagework in practice. Particularly useful is Cushway and Sewell's (1992) book which is also very relevant to groupwork practitioners. Rowan's (1993) work on the transpersonal approach in psychotherapy and counselling also contains a useful section on working with dreams, and much of his material on imagework is directly transferable to dreamwork.

Counselling

The use of dream and imagework as part of counselling should become part of good counselling practice and counsellors can learn how to value and work with their clients' personal imagery. Counsellors need to develop a sensitivity and respect for such material that is best developed through first becoming familiar with working on their own personal imagery. Counsellors need to be able to facilitate their clients' telling of their dream and can use many of the techniques to be outlined in the next chapter. The chapters already presented on the psychological and social anthropological perspectives on dreaming provide a theoretical basis for approaching dream and imagework. Overall this book intends to sensitise the interested practioner to the value of dreamwork with clients, patients and service users.

Oaklander has written about her use of dream and imagery work with children. She writes:

In general, dreams serve a variety of functions for children. They may be an expression of anxiety - things that worry them. They may express feelings that children feel unable to express in real life. They may depict wishes, wants, needs, fantasies, questions and curiosities, attitudes. The dream can be an indication of a general stance or feeling about life. It may be a way of working through feelings and experiences - situations that children are unable to deal with directly and openly (1969,p.150).

A major value of the studies summarised in this chapter is that the therapist, counsellor, nurse etc. can begin to become aware that dream imagery can be patterned in relation to personal and social change in the client/patient environment. A good example of this patterning of dream imagery is presented by the Zaya's (1988) study of the manifest dream imagery of expectant fathers. This study found that the dream imagery of expectant fathers typically went through three developmental stages which correlated temporally to the developing pregnancy. Whilst the sample of ten middle-class men is clearly very small and the analysis of dream content was made without reference to the fathers' studied, the study found the following progression. In the first stage the dream imagery seemed to reflect a concern with the man's workplace and also a sense of awe and curiosity with the creative space of the womb. In the second stage feelings of being excluded became manifest as well as a perception that the child was not yet identifiable as a person. In the third stage the amount of work-related dream content diminished significantly and there was more imagery concerning participation in family life. Also there was an increase in concern for their partner's and child's future health. Zaya writes that the findings show, 'the unconscious preoccupation of fathers represented symbolically in dreams' (Zaya, 1988). This example from the reported dreams of expectant fathers shows the potential value of using dreams as part of the assessment and intervention in the counselling process. The elaboration and definition of culturally-specific imaginative and emotional processes working through dream imagery would be a resource with which counsellors could work. In an analogous way to the stages of grief work that Kubler-Ross identified, perhaps dreamwork studies will similarily alert therapeutic practitioners to normal and abnormal change and adjustment processes.

The dream in groupwork practice

The following chapter, and indeed material throughout this book, will provide extensive examples of using groupwork methods with dreams. The works already referred to by Cushway and Sewell (1992), Ernst and Goodison (1981), Shohet (1985), Ullman, and Zimmerman (1979) and Ullman (1989), and Williams (1984) all provide useful and usually similiar guidance to both counsellors and groupwork practitioners. Oaklander (1969, p.147) usefully, but briefly, reports on the results of her group dreamwork with children. I (Edgar, 1992) have also written separately about using the dream as part of groupwork practice, and my findings are incorporated throughout this book.

Family therapy and dreamwork

Buchholz (1990) analyses two examples of using dream material in family therapy situations. He encountered a deep level of mutual understanding of dreams within these families. In the first example both the 18 year old boy, Billy, and his father had had the same dream in which Billy was pursued out of a cellar by a witch figure. Discussion of this dream image opened up key dynamics within the family linking Billy's drug addiction to his relationship to his parents and to the relationship between them. The 'witch' image was chronologically and dynamically linked to an early description of Billy's mother by her mother-in-law as being a 'witch', and overall the dream was understood in the session as expressing Billy's wish to escape a seductive mother-figure. The negative meaning ascribed to the 'witch' image in the discussion about the dream is presented in the article as being unproblematic. This 'witch' image appears to have been a key for both the male and female members of this family to share deep fears and fantasy material about each other. At the end of the session the father is reported as revealing that he in fact had been having an identical recurrent dream.

48

Interestingly, such a negative stereotyping or interpretation of the 'witch' image can be critiqued from a feminist perspective as being a deeply sexist interpretation. Such a conflictual diversity of interpretation well illustrates the micro-cultural and political aspects of contemporary dreamwork. The theme of the politics of dreamwork is continued in chapter eight.

The second dream image that Buchholz reports working with in his sessions is that of a suicidal girl who dreams of a 'broken egg in a nest' that she couldn't throw away. During this session the father emotionally identified the egg with his daughter and through the ensuing process of association and interpretation revelation about violence in the family was disclosed. The symbol of the 'broken egg in a nest' was shown to relate to the girl's frailty and the problem of self reconstruction she was facing. Buchholz suggests that such dream imagery is not solely the personal possession of the individual but represents the concretisation of the family's history and psychological state. Furthermore he writes that through this dreamwork the girl was enabled to recognise herself as an 'authoress' within the family situation.

Supervision, team building and dreamwork

Dreamwork has been used as part of the supervision process in one to one situations. Darou (1990) reports on his use of dreams in the supervision process. He provides case-material illustrating this use as well as pointing out how the issue of power inequality between supervisor and supervisee could be a major barrier to dream and/or associative content disclosure. He recommends this method only where a trusting relationship already exists between supervisor and supervisee. However, notwithstanding the potential problem of power inequality, he found that the use of dreams led speedily to core issues concerning the supervisee's work with clients, the team situation and possible transference material. He concludes that an experienced supervisor can quickly learn how to work with dreams from the available books and that dreamwork is a natural addition to supervision practice, though not yet a field taught in appropriate curricula. Whilst Darou worked one-to-one in the supervision relationship, I have recently used dream and imagework as part of a team-building process. Whilst this material has not yet been analysed, I found that working with a mixed gender, multi-professional health sector staff group could be successful given the commitment of the staff group. The group in question usually numbered six people and there was little hesitation by participants in taking spontaneous turns in recounting a recent dream. Clearly the group had basic trust in one another and notwithstanding the presence of their 'team leader', participants developed an openness with each other which allowed a considerable and sometimes surprising degree of personal sharing. Members reported that being in a dreamwork group had assisted in their remembering dreams and had validated the use of dreams. Moreover some members began to take the reported dreams of clients seriously and their reflective conjoint discussion of such imagery contributed to both assessment and intervention outcomes.

Conclusion

Overall this chapter has intended to show the considerable variety of professional therapeutic and empowerment settings in which dream and imagework can be used. Also I have indicated areas of dream research which illustrate possible patterns in dream imagery which can inform professional assessment and intervention. The field of 'social dreaming' will be developed in chapter eight.

5 Methods of working with dreams

Introduction

This chapter will present the varied groupwork-based methods used in the groups and illustrate, with case examples, the process by which these methods facilitated the evocation of meaning from dream and day imagery. The methods used by the group included: discussion and personal contextualisation; member suggestion; pair and small groupwork; gestalt and psychodrama; artwork and imagework; symbol amplification (dream re-entry); meditation. I will present the the use of binary analysis as an implicit part of the group reflective process. Binary analysis has already been introduced in chapter three and will be illustrated in this chapter. This chapter particularly illustrates and sets out the processes of cultural creativity applied to dream narration in the groups. A recent validation of social anthropology as offering a study of cultural creativity, rather than an exclusive concern with the application of abstract theory, is made by Charsley in his study of the cultural history of wedding cakes (1992, p.5). I intend that the material in this chapter shows the actual movement from 'nonsense' to 'sense' for the dreamer/narrator. The cultural and processual creation of meaning is evident in many of the following examples. After the narration of the dream the narrator experiences, on occasions, the evocation of meaning which is satisfactory and relevant to her/him. Satisfactory meaning can be seen to resonate within the identity and through the memory of the member as they choose to follow one or other interpretive pathway opened up by the group process.

If culture is the ascription and negotiation of meaning to everyday events, then dreamwork, and particularly the use of action techniques within the group context, such as gestalt and psychodrama, illustrate in an exemplary way the processual, interactive and negotiated nature of cultural creativity. Moreover, what is significant as we review this verbal and affective generation of meaning is how meaning and the ability to make connections between external events and internal imagery (memory and imagination) is often buried and repressed within the body of the person, that is the 'socially informed body' (Bourdieu, 1977, p.124). Bourdieu's work illuminates the way in which the body contains implicit knowledge. He shows how social values are retained and contained in the posture, gait and gaze of their possessors. It is no accident that totalitarian institutions spend so long inculcating cultural forms like British boarding schools in their emphasis on 'good manners'. The body is then 'treated as a memory' and:

> The principles em-bodied in this way are placed beyond the grasp of consciousness, and hence cannot even be made explicit; nothing seems more ineffable, more incommunicable, more inimitable, and therefore, more precious, than the values given body, *made* body by the transubstantiation achieved by the hidden persuasion of an implicit pedagogy, capable of instilling a whole cosmology, an ethic, a metaphysic, a political philosophy, through injunctions as insignificant as "stand up straight" or "don't hold your knife in your left hand (1977, p.94).

In this chapter I aim to show how group process and groupwork method can reveal the 'implicit' and repressed knowledge of the self. In this way Bourdieu's concepts, particularly of the body, explain how the social is written into all aspects of our lives and so provides a conceptual link between the 'worlds' of humanistic groupwork methodology and the social sciences.

Suggestion

Suggestion effectively means the ability of a member to ask the dream narrator for either further information or to 'suggest' looking at the dream or a part of it in a particular way. Any question in the form of, 'what colour was ...?' or 'how did you feel when?' or, 'how do feel now about..?' or, 'have you considered how X might relate to Y in your daytime life?' includes both a question being asked for more information, to flesh out the narrative, and also 'suggests' a possible avenue for enquiry by the dreamer. Suggestion can be more directive and 'suggestive'. For example in a dream where the dreamer had dreamt of having a baby, in contradistinction to her daytime intention, a group member asked her the question, 'What do babies mean to you?' and the dream narrator replied, 'Love, food, too much responsibility'. Sometimes the suggestion made is very directive as in the following example. A male dreamer has the following dream:

I was in a shop that I couldn't get out of...I was stuck...the customers wouldn't go...they kept coming in...it was five o'clock...I was trying to push them out and lock the door...and they wouldn't go...(now he says the dream is fairly easy to understand)*...the dream led into there being* *two couples...I was on holiday in America I think...there were two men and women...I was one of the men...I didn't know the others...I had some exams to revise for on Monday and the dream was on Friday but I was inveigled into going on this trip and I went...I had to go through the customs...and there was a desk in the sand and all the bureaucracy and I put down a document dated the thirtieth of November...Customs officer said 'this is out of date...you can't go'...by this time the other three had gone on...one women was walking off the boat and I waved and shouted 'hey this sod won't let me go through and I will have to go back' and they just walked on looking over their shoulders and then the man on the table just disappeared and I thought I can go now and I ran out and the boat has gone.*

Y. *Perhaps the boat leaving and your being missed was your wish not to take responsibility for decision-making...the women went and the decision was made for you.*

D. *That is the situation to a T! Also I thought there I am stopped officially and I am saying "I am coming back" and the decision is taken out of my hands.*

This example shows an interpretive suggestion being made by a group member, based on their extensive knowledge of the person's life situation. In this case the interpretation was accepted, but this was not always the case.

Discussion and personal contextualisation

The ability of the group to perform 'successful' dreamwork depended on members' self-disclosing and, in particular, on the narrator of the dream giving contextual information about current and past events in their life. In the following dream the symbolism is about 'moving house'. The female dreamer begins by saying the dream takes her back into scary feelings; she tells the dream as a story. She can see parallels with her own life:

It is a mix of things...real and other people's doing...I go to my parent's house...I haven't lived there long...Mother tells me she is going to move...I am quite surprised...mother says to father...'you are getting old...You will have to stop all this physical work around the house'...the back garden is in complete disarray...they are digging up paving stones in their paved garden...they don't know where they are going...they have no other place...I feel confused...they seem crazy to be digging up the paving stones and to be moving...I decide to go along with it...I don't feel it would achieve anything by discussion...mother is being very angry about digging up the paving stones...I am helping...I am sifting through the fibrous soil and taking out bulbs...I am not leaving anything behind.

53

The narrator then continues to give information about her life that is clearly vital for any attempt to understand the dream imagery:

*This dream occurred the day after my house was put up for sale...therefore the material is half real! I have lived in this house for many years and I have brought up a child in it...*She then talks about moving from her own house and about how very panicky and insecure she now feels. *I have a much stronger reaction than I imagined...I am shaken...I am having these feelings as I am talking...I feel fear and uncertainty...*She tells how she remembers how she got to her house, *it is the first place I have felt secure in...previously my accommodation has been rented...my parents are alive and are not moving...it is a bizarre idea that they should be moving...they are very rooted...my parents have lived in their present house for X years and before that in a house where I grew up for Y years...my parents view of me is that 'she' is always doing unpredictable things...its just her...another crazy thing! I feel my house is an anchor...It feels really scarey...I can't pull up the anchor until I can sell the house...I can't do something new...In the dream there were bulbs...my parents wanted to move everything with them. even the bulbs.*

In this example, perhaps surprisingly from the first session of the first group, the dreamer gives considerable personal biographical information to the group. In this example the information allows the group to focus on the dream imagery as being likely to represent, albeit in a changed and distorted form, the dreamer's feelings aroused by her proposed house sale. The feelings of 'being uprooted' are later described in the gestalt section in this chapter. In the following discussion of a dream we can see the evocative process between suggestion and insight that leads to a set of understandings about the dream by the dreamer:

I stayed in bed one morning...it's only a snatch of a dream ...its about my teeth...they are not a constant anxiety but I do have a fear of having my front teeth smashed...I do have crowns that I am self conscious of...the dentist in the dream has put new teeth on...so I feel relief that I shall have teeth to cover the gaps...then I look in the mirror and I see they are my mother's teeth...when I look in the mirror I realise they are greyer...this seems okay for a while till I realise that the new teeth are much greyer which will show people that the original teeth were crowns too.

The following is an edited version of the ensuing discussion. D is the dream narrator:

D.*I am thinking about being without teeth...about being raw and exposed and about people knowing there is something false about you.*

54

Q. *Did she bite?*

D. *Its not about biting...The dentist knew they were mother's teeth...my relationship with my mother is okay but distant...usually dreaming about teeth is about your own ageing...typically teeth falling out is about ageing...there's a lot about image and about being real...I had a fear of breaking my teeth and it did happen...I had an X accident and I lost my front teeth...Lots of people visited and I was freaked about not having any teeth...Why this fear about not having teeth? It must mean something about not taking care of myself and as it was an accident it was okay to have lost them.*

The narrator then talks about the ugliness of having no teeth:

D. *Something is rotting.*

Q. *Like being a toothless hag.*

D. *Yes...I was glad to have my mother's teeth rather than being toothless...it feels sad to have ended up with something not quite right...I remember my mother taking her denture out of her mouth and cleaning it...I didn't want my mother's teeth...I want my own teeth undamaged...there is something about pretence...it was a double pretence ...as I had had the crowns first.*

Q. *What is being covered up?*

D. (laughs) *It's about not being truthful...about pretending to be something that I'm not...pretending to be more whole...more perfect than I am.*

Q *Putting on a good front.*

D. *That really fits in with work...It's about the front...about pretending to be together...its about this job I am supposed to be doing...I haven't been feeling together at all dealing with everyone else in emotional crisis.*

Q. *It's about being strong*

D. *At work it's about me taking care of everyone else...and who takes care of me?*

D. talks about her feeling of pretending and of *'being strong'* at work. There is nowhere at work for her to explore this...nowhere for her to get attention:

D. *There is a limit to how long I can go on putting up the pretence...I have had a real battle getting the management to realise that workers needed their own support...I feel the management had not been supportive or understanding of these needs...sometimes I blame myself and think that I ought to be able to manage.*

K. *I Feel D has had to wear it (the mask) for everyone else...like you are wearing the teeth...you are wearing it for everyone else in the workplace.*

55

Z. *You are the only one being 'shown up'* (like teeth).
D. *That is exactly like it is...I feel I am carrying it for the 'consumers' and in order to get the situation changed I have had to be very real about myself...and with people who I haven't felt responded sympathetically.*
Q. *You have to be mother?*
D. *Yes...I have to be mother to the whole fucking world...that's what it feels like...and yet I don't know how to stop.*
J. *The image of biting is coming across for me...that is the opposite of nurturing...softness.*
A. *Its like the nurturing I am really missing... I am also not being very caring about myself...but there is this sudden surge of anger...it is the resentment about giving out and not getting back...and the lack of response from other people.*

D. then talks about the dentist and her feeling that she is receiving second best concerning the teeth in the dream:

Q. *Just like in the organisation.*
D. *They're not good enough...both the teeth and the work support are pretty shoddy...second best...shoddy...it fits but it's not very good.*

Then D. talks about not being happy in general at work and a member suggests the 'mother's' teeth are invasive in some way:

D. *What I can pick up there is the invasive bit...about boundaries...I feel really overwhelmed and there is nowhere for me to go...a friend is staying with me and had made dramatic disclosures about their Y. (reference changed)...also someone I know has been attacked (reference changed) this symbolised the last straw for me...so the invasiveness bit symbolised for me the awful side of humanity...it seems to be overwhelming and I am feeling overwhelmed by it.*
Z. *How can we resolve this within the time and prepare D for leaving the group this evening?*
D. *As I think about it I feel angry about it and don't think it is good enough...I am angry...it is quite hard for me to be angry...I feel it is difficult to confront...to say I want and I deserve something better...I feel he (the dentist) is doing his best but it is not good enough.*

D. then speaks to the 'dentist' as in a gestalt exercise:

D. *I don't trust you enough to really give me some nice teeth I want some really splendid teeth...I can have the best crowns in the world.*
U. *Are you going to ask him to do it or go somewhere else.*
D. *I don't trust him but it feels really threatening to go somewhere else and to start all over again and to take this big risk...and all these*

56

dentists are men! my real dentist is very nice...so its about not settling for things that aren't good enough.

In this discussion about the 'meaning' of the dream and of how the imagery may relate to 'reality' there is a process of question and suggestion and development of insight for the dreamer. This is not purely a result of suggestion by group members, as is shown at the beginning by the dreamer rejecting the avenue of enquiry suggested by the question 'Did she bite?' The dreamer knows about the 'typical' connection of teeth with ageing but doesn't exactly pursue that theme in relation to her own ageing process. Rather she connects the imposition of the teeth with the loss of teeth in an accident and particularly focuses on the theme of the 'falsity' of the teeth. Then she talks about falsity and in response to a question about 'what is being covered up?' talks about putting on a 'front' at work. The idea of a 'front' is suggested by a member and the dreamer says that really 'fits in with work'. The next stage sees the dreamer sharing her perception that she is 'being strong' for other people at work, particularly other workers. The 'teeth' symbol now is explicitly connected with that of the 'mask' or 'persona'. In response to the question 'you have to be mother?', the dreamer replies, 'Yes I have to be mother to the whole fucking world'. The dreamer here is identifying with the 'motherness' of the teeth being inserted into her mouth in the dream and recognising that that is how she feels in her work setting. Following a suggestion that 'boundaries are being invaded' (i.e. mother's false teeth in her mouth), the final level of interpretation reached is that feelings of being overwhelmed by events in the world, the patriarchal world, are manifest. Feelings of anger are articulated and finally the dreamer is facilitated to affirm her 'first class' value and her right to have first class teeth fitted.

This example illustrates very well the progression of insight through different levels in response to suggestion and interpretive questioning. There is a transformation of the image of the 'teeth' to their being seen as representing the 'front' or 'persona' (originally the persona was a Jungian formulation). The word 'persona' then is expanded to refer to 'mothering', perhaps 'inappropriate mothering', and finally, the identification with 'mothering' changes to a feminist articulation of anger at patriarhical abuse. Resolution is achieved through self-affirmation.

Any of these levels of insight, which expand in terms of scope of reference from the personal to the global, could be seen by the group as equating with 'meaning' for the dreamer. 'Sense' then has been derived from the 'nonsense' of the dream. A series of themes, connected to life events, have been derived from images. The interpretation of the 'teeth' image is through reference to biographical data and to the physical context of the teeth as being in the 'front' of the mouth; being a 'social front' to others as well as being a functional piece of equipment for the mastication of food. In that sense the understanding of the 'teeth' symbol relies on a public and culturally specific symbolism that evaluates the significance of teeth, and particularly the gendered nature of 'attractive' teeth, in certain ways. Our teeth are perceived in Westernised culture as being a part, and a very important part as evidenced by the amount of cosmetic dentistry, of our social front to the world. The social construction of our teeth as a 'dental object' has recently been analysed by Nettleton (1992, p.18-28). The 'mother' image in this dream and its discussion are again personally contextualised. The dreamer states that 'her relationship with her mother is okay'. Hence that possible avenue for exploration is not pursued. The 'mother' symbol instead is connected with her 'overwhelming' set of feelings of responsibility for others, particularly in her workplace. The 'mother' symbol is identified with care and responsibility for others, and it is critically interpreted as not being a fulfilling aspect of herself but rather as an an inappropriately acquired set of responses which she would like to divest herself of. Feeling like being a 'mother' to the 'whole fucking world' is a problem to her.

There is a translation here from a reference to the personal mother to the 'archetypal' mother as Jung (1959, p.81) defines the 'mother archetype'. As Jung states, all archetypes have a potentially positive and negative aspect and here we can see a negative, or partly negative, rendering of that set of feelings and roles identifying this archetype for the dreamer. We see here then the dreamer concluding with a feminist critique of herself for coming to adopt such a 'false' persona and for identifying with such an inappropriate 'mother' role in relation to the world. However her self criticism is deflected, expanded and refocused into a generalised anger with the abuse and rapacity of the male in this society. The conclusion is self assertive and affirms her autonomous selfhood and her rights to the best. The socially constructed transformative and evocative process hinges on a series of transformations engendered by the interaction of the dreamer with the group: teeth = front = mothering = lack of self care = anger at men = affirmation of self.

Pair and small group work

The group split itself into pairs and small groups of three or four people on three occasions. Pair work allows the opportunity for greater self-disclosure and is particularly effective at the beginning of a group to facilitate personal sharing. However I made no attempt to audio-record any pair or small group because of the obvious problems of noise and the need for several recorders. The significance of pairwork for this discussion is that the setting is made more intimate, otherwise the group and social processes are the same, though more restricted in terms of the use of drama. One example of the development of greater self-disclosure through small groupwork is when three female members all shared dreams with faeces imagery in them. They further said that it was only because of the size and shared gender of the small group that they disclosed this imagery.

58

Group member association

As already indicated in the chapter on the group process, member association with the dreamer's narrated imagery was a two edged affair. Whilst an empathic understanding and identification with the imagery and with the possible meaning for the dreamer was perceived as supportive and developmental, as is shown in the last 'teeth' example, the reverse could be true. Members could 'jump in' with their own associations and projections and thereby confuse the process for the dreamer. This was a group 'problem' discussed and addressed in terms of needing to 'respect the dream'.

In the group the practice was developed of introducing a possible line of enquiry and suggestion by the phrase, 'if that was my dream I ....'. Such an approach is also recommended by Ullman and Zimmerman (1979), and Cushway and Sewell (1992). Also, as I will discuss in the next chapter on the group, the question of sexual projection by a member onto a dream image was an issue for the group. Occasionally there seemed little connection between the dream imagery and the resulting interpretive and supportive discussion. For example the following is another 'tooth' dream:

In church at choir practice there is the vicar and me and two other singers and I am waiting for it to start...perhaps other people are still to come...and I am clenching and unclenching my jaw...like that and I am aware that there is a filling in a bottom molar and there is a filling in a top molar and they are touching...and then I am aware that there is a piece of metal coming down..(T. starts crying a bit) *and um it actually comes down and gets trapped in the bottom one and I am still clenching and unclenching my jaw...and I am almost tempting fate doing it tighter every time to see if a hook of metal is going to trap into the bottom molar and to do this and sure enough I do it till they lock together and the only way I can open my jaw is by pulling out the bottom filling and I sort of go...*(makes noises) *and the tooth underneath crumbles and the whole mouth feels full of bits...and I am leaving the church and going into a small room and I look in the mirror...and there is a huge filling in a load of bits and then a few hours later...I have a sense of a few hours later...there are still a few bits of tooth coming out and it feels just horrible and the tension is just horrible and I have this thing about metal in my mouth and I had an earlier dream about silver foil in my mouth and it is not the physical pain it is the tension...waiting almost for a physical shock.*

There followed a clarifying discussion. T. represents the dreamer. A short gestalt exercise followed and involved the dreamer identifying with 'feeling what it was like being her mouth'.

A member asks about the isue of 'fault' saying:

A. It (tightening her jaw till the tooth crumbles) *seems to be what you wanted...you were testing it out and it was your fault you brought it on yourself.*

T. This time yes...not always in the other ones (previous similar dreams).

Then the dreamer is offered the opportunity 'to be the crumbly teeth'. She doesn't want to do this. and another member 'doubles' (note 1) and so acts as if she was the dreamer: TT. is the 'double' of the dreamer (T.).

TT. I am falling out...I am losing my grip and I am very insecure and wobbly and my contact with the living tissue...stop me if this isn't right...I am falling about into T's mouth...and I have given up...I am useless.

T. Thank you it is really helpful to see...the thing I find really hard is the metal and the hardness of the tooth and the softness of the mouth and that really shakes me and sets my teeth on edge.

X. It's harder and shouldn't be there and is out of place.

T. Something shakes my whole being and it is the whole idea of eating chewing gum and a friend coming up and chewing onto the frame of your teeth and expecting it to be soft...it is the hard/soft thing...really horrible.

Y. There is no pain around this is there?

T. Not the physical pain it is the trauma...same with the foil on the tooth...its not the pain it is....(She becomes silent)

X. Things seem insecure with your teeth falling out...and any minute something is going to happen.

T. You are almost tensing your self for something to happen.

P. It is as if it is an alien body in the softness of your mouth that shouldn't be there...it's like you are putting it to its final test...to see what it is going to feel like and I am wondering where this hook is coming from.

T. It came out of the filling...there is a hook in the top molar...it sort of grew coming down and it was very small (she demonstrates).

Y. What made you cry.

T. When I was talking about the metal in the tooth. T is still shuddering and upset.

P. Do you want to look at these two sides of yourself...the hard and the soft.

T. I recognise I have both sides in me...over the last few months I have come to terms with the darker side of me and recognising it ...giving it more space like the soft side...saying 'we love one another don't we ?' ...I have been angry and voiced more difficult things than usual...is this the soft/hard thing?...yes...as the soft is the more accommodating side and the hard side says no...actually that has pissed me off for many years...I was afraid to express feelings that weren't positive and

60

*it is new to feel that that is alright and that I can relate to the hard
and the soft...the accommodating and the not accommodating sides.*

I. *That is rational but what about the horror of the metal in the
teeth...can you associate the picture with anything else outside?*

T. *I made a connection yesterday...the night before the dream I had an
experience of some boys barring the way whilst I was cycling and one
of them grabbed my bum...and today I made this connection and I
was happily cycling along and I saw these four boys and I went
headlong into the situation...and afterwards I was quite shaken...I had
to get down off the bike and I felt quite vulnerable...and that has
shaken me and then I had the dream that night.*

F. *You said you should have foreseen it.*

T. *I was talking about it and I felt I wasn't to blame and I was really
angry about it* (crying still a bit) *why should I have to look out all the
time why can't I just feel open.*

A member then suggests that she is making a connection between the
'fault' in her tooth dream and the real life threatening incident. The dreamer
says she is not sure if the two are related.

T. *I'm not sure if the dream is related to this incident.*

Here the dreamer voices her concern that the possibly interpretive
connection is illusory. The dialogue continues:

Q. *The mouth mirrors the vagina...tthink of the tongs they use and the
stitches...there is a connection with your bum that they got hold off.*

I. *Holding the bum is an invasion of your body...an assault...I can feel a
lot of anger and guilt around that that has been around for a long
time with you...you would have felt the incident was your fault.*

Q. *Is guilt the hook?*

H. *Åre you hooked on guilt?*

There is no affirmation by T. of this.

Q. Talks about as a nurse how: *you feel responsible for their sexual
harassment.*

T. Talks about why feeling so: *vulnerable when they are only thirteen
year olds...when I am really shaken it is my teeth that shake with fear
hence the connection between fear of boys and tooth dream?*

I. *So the teeth are 'on guard' like a portcullis.*

T. then talks about her recurrent dreams i.e. a horrible dream drinking
champagne and glass shattering in her mouth and she keep picking bits out.
Then the dreamer, deciding to 'work' on this interpretive avenue, elects to

61

act out her feelings and speak to the harassing boys and uses a cushion to express her feelings in a cathartic way. Other members 'double' for her:

F. Shouts at the boys (role-playing 'being T'), *fuck off go away leave me alone get your filthy paws off my bum.*

T. Says they will carry on *'daring'* (to invade her space).

T. (in tears), *I don't feel strong enough...I still feel too small and vulnerable.*

T. (coming out of the drama by now), *I feel when you two are speaking that it is penetratingly real and I want to speak at them like that but I don't have the strength to say ...but it feels very real and if I put it in my mouth it will...I will crumble.* Another member suggests to T. *can you tell those boys quietly what you feel.*

T. Does this.

P. Becomes the boys saying (as boys): *We had a good laugh...you looked really cute coming along there.*

T. *I am not here to look cute for you I am just here to live my life...I should be able to do what I want.*

P. *I didn't mean you any harm ...it was a good laugh.*

T. *But you intruded.*

The discussion continues with the expression of anger towards such kids and then a discussion of how women can protect themselves from such verbal and physical harassment.

Binary analysis of dream report

The group in this example develops an embryonic structuralist analysis consisting of oppositions linked by analogy and homology. Structuralist theory has used binary analysis (Fox,1975 p.99) as an analytic device. Binary analysis is a way of reducing and organising the cultural complexity that confronts anthropologists when analysing or comparing societies. Structural analysis, such as in Lévi-Strauss's story of Asdiwal (1976, p.146), posits certain structured logical features underlying cultural activity and conceptualisation. These are deemed to be universal to all cultures. In the 'Mythologies' Lévi-Strauss (1970, p.10) seeks to establish a framework of 'laws' determining mythical creation in human society. Part of this logical structure is the analogous sequence of paired oppositions. Among the most commonly found sets are, heaven: earth; raw:cooked; sacred:profane; and male:female. These binary oppositions are connected into a system by the principle of analogy (Leach, 1970, p.27). For example Needham suggests that these oppositions:

..need not be connected by qualitative resemblances between individual terms, but instead they are connected as homologues (a:c and b:c) in a classification by analogy...(1979, p.66).

Such constructions claiming to reflect the universal features of human understanding are open to criticism about their usefulness. Sperber writes that such anthropology is in danger of having, 'constructed a structural model without an object' (1975, p.68). Leach (1970, p.53) also later questioned the usefulness of the approach of binary analysis and Douglas (1975, p.250) is critical of Lévi-Strauss's reliance on binary analysis Certainly anthropology can use binary analysis to organise cultural phenomena into an identifiable pattern or formal model. Yet the conclusions drawn can vary. Needham writes that the only test of a successful model is: 'the degree of success in rendering social facts coherent and intelligible' (1979, pp.58-59). An admirable example of the use of binary analysis as a part of a cultural analysis of dream is Carrither's (1982, pp.29-45) study of the dreams of a monk in Sinhalese culture. In his analysis, which relies extensively on binary analysis as an ordering and classificatory device, he shows how the monk both dreamt within the religious imagery of the Buddhist order, of which he was a member, and also understood this imagery through the lens of Buddhist morality and religious cosmology.

I use binary analysis as a way of structuring and making intelligible the interpretive flow of the above discussion. The appropriateness of such an analysis at this point is due to its resonance with the way that the narrator and the group began to structure their explanations and associations to the narrated dream imagery. The extended example above again shows several interpretive processes occurring in the group. In the first part there is the connection, facilitated by the group, of the imagery of the dream in a subjective way. The imagery is thought to refer to the duality or set of opposites within the personality of the dreamer. The key opposition is that of hard: soft. Within the discussion of the dream imagery, the opposition between the hard teeth and soft tissue is developed; there is the opposition between natural and unnatural in which the 'natural' is the tooth and the 'unnatural' is the metal filling. The opposition between the soft mouth and hard tooth is developed by an invitation from a group member for the dreamer to look at that opposition with reference to their being two sides of herself, the soft and the hard side. The dreamer interprets this opposition in terms of the tension between the loving, caring and nurturing side and the assertive side that is able to deal with conflict and can voice difficult feelings:

....the soft is the more accommodating side and the hard side says no!...I was afraid to express feelings that weren't positive...I can relate to the hard and the soft...the accommodating and the not accommodating sides.

The dreamer re-expresses this opposition in terms of 'accommodating' and 'not accommodating'. At this point the dreamer declares a possible connection between the dream imagery of that night and the harassing experience of the day before. At first she declares that this connection may not really be related to the imagery, there being no clear 'hook' for the projection. However shortly after she identifies the connection in terms of her feeling that her teeth shake with fear, and this gives her the connection between 'teeth' and the frightening experience of the day before. With this information the group leaves the previous interpretive format, a more gestalt mode, and take a more social and political, even feminist stance in relation to reclaiming physical space, not dental space, for all people and particularly women. I further develop a political approach to dreamwork in chapter eight. The 'crumbling teeth' which appears at one point to become a metaphor for her current non-assertive and 'crumbling self' are turned in the ensuing role-play into an assertive voice in her mouth claiming her rights and exposing her criticism of the boys. Further oppositions have then emerged, particularly those between male: female; and danger: safety. The opposition between inside : outside becomes an analogy at two levels, between that of the accommodating self : the non-accommodating self and also the feminist : non-feminist self; passivity and assertiveness are also being polarised. However the opposition inside : outside also resonates with the possibilities of a subjective : objective interpretive reference for this dream. Overall we see then an emerging system of binary classification, partly articulated by members. I present these in the following table:

Table 1: Table of oppositions

Soft mouth : hard metal
Natural : unnatural.
Soft nature : hard nature.
Accommodating disposition : Non-accommodating disposition.
Inside : outside.
Crumbling : hard.
Female : male.
Feminist : non-feminist.
Internal referents : external referents.
Psyche : world.

This set of oppositions, linked by homology and analogy (Needham, 1979, p.66), are evident in the text. Yet change in attitude and the affirmation of the self are being enacted in this dramatic restaging of a crumbling mouth and a harassing incident. The soft passive and non-assertive accommodating self is being changed into an assertive self. In the individual interview with this member, after the groups, in answer to the question, *Has the group affected your life?* she said, *Oh yes, particularly my reaction to conflict...it has underlined my avoidance of conflict...and made me value confronting conflict.* This dream narration and discussion show several important features along with that of the issue of how a dreamer associates or projects onto their imagery both before and during the narration and discussion of the dream. This example also shows the implicit and beginning development of a structuralist analysis of the dream text by the group, and included within that text, the set of external referents identified by the dreamer with the aid of the group.

Gestalt

The theory and method of gestalt has already been introduced with an example in chapter two, and in the previous example in this chapter a gestalt exercise was used. As the gestalt method used was such an important and frequent process I will give two further examples, plus an additional example of a form of group gestalt. In the following bulb example I will present the gestalt exercise and the ensuing discussion.

The dream of bulbs has already been presented earlier in this chapter, in the section on discussion and personal contextualisation, and relates to the dreamer's parents moving house. In the gestalt exercise the dreamer (F) is encouraged to be the 'bulb(s)' that at the end of the dream are being dug up by her parents. In her memory of the dream this is a relatively insignificant part of the dream. The transcript includes questions and suggestions from the group as to ways of understanding the dream imagery:

> F. *I am a bulb...I'm rather a nice shape...full of nourishment...food for the future...a bit magical...I go into the ground...stay in the ground...through the winter...just in the ground...suddenly it is spring...I really grow...emerge spectacular...absolutely incredible...splash of colour...bright vivid colours...really beautiful after the winter...I.make a spectacular display...it's really good* (emphasised).
>
> I. *How do you feel about being dug up?*
>
> F. *I feel really scared...there are no roots only a bare base...I feel a bit sick at the thought of being dug up...I have only a brown paper coating...it's a bit yellow...layers taken off.*
>
> I. *How do you feel about mother?*
>
> F. *I don't feel secure with mother...I don't know why she is digging me up...I have no sense of being taken care of...it's a bit brutal...I don't know where I am going to go...will I grow as well? Its very threatening.*
>
> D. *I have a sense of your having been in the ground a long time...of your losing your roots...of feeling a bit forgotten...of not having slabs on top...slabs are like tombstones.*
>
> I. *Where do you want to be?*

F. I don't want to be in the garden...I want to be somewhere more open with no garden wall/fence...I want to be in a grassy area...so when I come up I've got a contrast with the colours...I want some space ...it would be quite nice to have some trees there...it feels quite safe with some trees there.

T. There would be really strong tree roots.

F. Yes...I would like some beech trees...They feel protective but not constricting...I would want some water...quite a large lake...I feel insecure...a bit bare-skinned...no brown paper...I have got to have my head and neck out...I don't want to be too deep underground...I want some air...not too deep in the dark ...if it is too deep I start to feel I am suffocating...I can't get my flowers and leaves up...I have a partnership with the soil...as long as I'm not buried too deep...we have a kind of truce.

Q. You have got a good relationship going! (laughter) *what do you do for the Summer?*

Later F. spoke about some of the issues that had come up for her through the exercise and begins by talking about her relationship with her mother.

F. I am trying to accept.the interdependence bit...I have fears about dependency and then I react the other way...I need to accept interdependence without being frightened of it being dependency...I couldn't bear the paving stones...I valued darkness and springing into colour.

X. Asks F. to explore, she who was digging you up.

F. I didn't feel protected...felt exposed...didn't feel safe...didn't know what she was doing...no sense...something precious being transported somewhere nice...the feeling of not being cared for was predominant.

X. She is not being kind to you in moving?

F. Not taking care of self.

Q. Not leaving anything behind.

F. It felt a destructive thing to be doing...this digging up...not taking care of things...like smashing...don't know why I felt angry.

F. Now talks about the house she lived in before her present house...*I had to leave...then I moved into my present house which was not where I wanted to be...I have a lot of anger about having to move...*(tape not clear) *there is a driven quality about mother...about her driving my father and me that fits in with how I see her.*

The above example well illustrates the dreamer's capacity to imaginatively identify with 'being a bulb'. She was able to 'get in touch' with a set of feelings about 'uprootedness' and began to articulate where, as a bulb, she would like to be. Her present feelings of vulnerability become manifest and the theme that emerges for her is the issue of dependence, independence and interdependence, particularly in relation to her parents. The identification with the bulb and the bulb's imagined relationship with the soil becomes, during the exercise, a lived symbol for the relationship between herself and her mother in particular. Whilst originally, in the dream and its narration, the bulb image had appeared unimportant, through this gestalt identification the bulb symbol had been 'grown' in the dreamer's mind and a range of perceptions and emotions triggered and experienced through participating in the exercise. In fact the bulb symbol was adopted the following week as the first visualisation exercise for the group, with powerful results from the identifications experienced.

Such a visual and affective identification by the dreamer/narrator with one or more of the dreamt and narrated symbols is typical of the process encountered in these groups. Another reality is being generated in the group session, as clearly the narrator 'knows' she is not in reality a bulb. Rather she is involved in a ritual evocation of a fantastical reality which she joins through the supportive work and facilitation of the group. Normal reality is suspended in the ritual space and time constructed by the group. The candlelight and softened atmosphere of the meeting encourages this suspension of reality. The dreamer and the group 'warm up' to this imagined reality. Buried feelings are allowed and encouraged to emerge and are approved by the group. 'Being a bulb' is a ritual transformation of the self, a play imaginatively enacted within the group space. She is not really a 'bulb' as she speaks as a 'human bulb' who *feels a bit sick at the thought of being dug up,* and who can again transform herself from the 'growing bulb' into the 'bulb being dug up by her mother' which is clearly a symbol for her relationship with her 'mother' in real life.

This is not a social discourse, a simple conversation with others about moving house and her relationship with her mother. The monologue and occasional dialogue has a different and ritual dimension. Evocation, invocation and identification flow through the spoken works. She starts, *I am a bulb...I am rather a nice shape...full of nourishment.* Such spoken sentiments articulate a profound metaphorisation and articulation of the self. The imaginative creations represent a spontaneous playing with metaphorical meaning and its possible relationship to normal reality. The choice of the bulb, derived from the dream image, is typically full of almost endless possibility. The bulb is the seed and it is her imagination, encouraged by the group, that develops this remembered image into a kind of mini-archetype and lived metaphor. This development of a lived or root metaphor allows the possibility of a transformative experience to be engendered. In this sense it is a ritual process and occasion that allows the evocative development of a symbol in a controlled and managed space. She becomes the bulb which in its changing place becomes her existential predicament of moving house and her unsatisfactory relationship with her mother. Indeed in this presented text we can see whole seasons pass by as in:

I go into the ground...stay in the ground through the winter...just in the ground...suddenly it is spring...I really grow...emerge spectacular...really beautiful after the winter.

Transformation then has occurred, feelings evoked and expressed and an imaginative change process facilitated. This text reports another reality which is taken seriously and encouraged by the group. Group members have played a central role in this movement, asking questions, making suggestions and repeating key phrases. The group is a significant part of the communicative context which enables an articulation of satisfactory and emergent meaning. The second example was a particularly powerful experience for the dreamer. The dream went as follows:

I had bought a car...a black one...I think a Ford Escort but I am not sure...I am very pleased with it...it is a good buy and the inside is very spacious...it has pineclad walls and windows as well...after a while something strange happened about this car...I realised it was a hearse (a significant transformation from car to hearse takes place here) *a converted hearse...and there is a body in it as well...hidden away in the roof...concealed and at some point it might slide down some kind of ramp...at first I don't recognise this body...it is in formal morning suit with top hat and striped trousers and that kind of stuff...that part of the dream stops there...and picks up with something more understandable to me in relation to my X. dying and so it switches to Y. place as my X. was born there and the ashes were returned there...In Y. I am at P. castle and I know we have to bury my X...and there is a salute you know when they fire the cannons at one o'clock...that happens and I look over the battlements and there is a red stone church or buildings close by and I know that is T. near where my X. was born and the scene switches there and there is some problem about doing the service for a few hours and meantime I discover there is only the first name on the coffin only ...there is only the first name on the coffin...I am really upset about that as it could be any such* (first name) *and it isn't and then I wonder what we are doing anyway burying X. as he has to be cremated and the dream goes onto something completely different and is unconnected and so it ends there.*

T. is the dreamer in the ensuing dialogue:

T. I woke up a bit like when you are a kid and a hearse drives by and it makes you feel superstitious about whether death is coming.
Q. Who was the body?
T. It wasn't my X. I think it was my husband because it had a (colour) *beard.*
F. You said the hearse was a good buy!

68

T. Yes I got that as well...I was certain it was a good buy...he had on the clothes he had on when we got married. Long silence for thirty seconds.

F. That sounds quite confused...you don't quite know where you are.

Q. Does your husband represent your father?

*T. No...he is I think...God it is complicated...I thought if he represented anything it would be...*she speaks very quietly here.

P. Has that aspect of you died?

T. It (that possible interpretation) *doesn't resonate.*

Here we see a tacking back and forth as possible meaning avenues are offered up for exploration by the group but the dreamer/narrator doesn't necessarily accept them. Rejection occurs when the the imaginative idea suggested, 'doesn't resonate'. This resonating or not resonating is controlled by the narrator as the only 'facts' in the situation are being conveyed and constructed by the narrator her/himself. S/he therefore controls the production of an acceptable narrative of the self.

F. Is it significant you are going on a journey?

P. Were you driving?

T. It was my car...I don't remember driving.

K. It feels an excitement about it...it is a gripping time.

*P. With pine cladding inside...*laughter.

T. It was very blond pine...I suppose it could be 'pining' (sounds as S has a sad insight here).

Q. It was a car with character.

T. A multifarious car.

Q. The car was you?

T. Yes.

D. You were sure it was a Ford Escort?

T. Yes I think so.

T. When I got it buying a car was a fairly liberating thing to do...When I missed (my husband) *away it was partly missing the car...I had to face that.*

F. When he was at home that was the 'death' of him!

I. It was an Escort?

T. You are going too fast for me.

*T. It was the death of him?...Oh right!...when he came home...*It takes a moment for the dreamer to connect with what was suggested.

F. You didn't really miss him?

F. If you were going to be something in the dream which bit would you pick.

T. I suppose the car.

F. Not the body.

T. No...no.

Q. How do feel as the car?

*T. Uhm I have a secret ...***Oh goodness me** *I am quite a flashy car...quite smart...I cut a good figure you know as cars go.*

I. Fast?

T. I don't like that one...I don't have a sense of speed...people are in awe of me but I don't really know why that is...I feel very kind of substantial.

F. What's it like...having a secret?

T. It's like its mine...something that belongs to me...it's quite powerful and precious as it belongs to me but it is getting quite heavy...the roof is not very strong...I don't know whether I can keep this secret going...it feels like there is lots of room inside...loads of space...quite bright and light but it is empty.

F. Where are you going?

T. Following my nose...I can see lots of different roads and I can go down any one of them.

Q. Is that body pressing down?

T. Yes a bit.

T. I am not like a hearse as I haven't declared the body...it's a secret.

T. People don't see me as a hearse...but I know I am.

T. (big sigh). *That's had quite a powerful effect...I feel I might be dangerous* (emphasised)*...it has more to do with what I seem to be and what I am...I am puzzled about that...I don't see myself as a hearse...so it upsets me that people behave as if I am normal.*

F. Do other people see you as a hearse. '

T. They see me as one...they do but I don't...people don't know about the dead body.

P. How do you feel about this body descending from you?

T. (sighs) *I am pleased it has gone...it's **ah.**.its the body that makes it a hearse...I don't like to be a hearse* (sighs, it is clearly difficult for her).

Q. You don't have to keep a secret anymore.

T. It doesn't matter about the secret.

F. What's going to happen to the body? you have completely got rid of it?...its gone...you have been carrying it a long time.

I. Do you want to say anything to the body?

T. (crying) *Yes...I would like to say a little bit...*(much sighing/silence). *You have got a beard.* G. acts as a body,

T. Puts a black jacket on the body.

T. I didn't know who you were... I didn't recognise you?

There are long silences and I didn't catch everything, but my notes say that it was about T. not loving him but he loving her; she spoke in a muted way but with no anger; said goodbye to him and let the body slide away. This was very emotional for her and the onlookers. *T.* says, *I felt I shouldn't have got married.*

In this dream narration and accompanying gestalt exercise, the theme of death is powerfully present with the image of a recently dead close relative and the car as a hearse with a dead body in it. The dreamer recognises that in the dream it is her husband who is the dead body in the hearse. A question allows the dreamer to confirm that *'the hearse was a good buy'*. The suggestion is made that the dreamer should consider whether the dead person represents some part of herself that has died. The dreamer rejects that subjective avenue. The cue to the 'interpretation' begins with the punning on the word 'pining'. The dreamer says she *'could be pining'*. It is unclear as to whether this is pining for herself or a part of her or a 'dead' relationship or an actually dead person. She is invited to pick a part of the dream imagery, to do a gestalt identification with it. She chooses the car image and straight away recognises that she has a secret and is apparently surprised that she is *'quite a flashy car... quite smart...cut a good figure'*. This identification with the car begins to reflect her self perception and she continues by musing on having a secret in the car. Then, although it was impossible to recognise it from the tape, she in her imagination, *'tips the body out of the hearse'*. At this point the dreamer becomes very upset after having shed the dead body of her husband. In the ensuing dialogue that she makes with the dead body she speaks tearfully and emotionally about lost love and the imbalance of love between them.

In this dream narration and gestalt exercise it is clear that unexpected and embodied emotions were raised for the dreamer and their articulation to the group was significant. In the individual interview the dreamer spoke about this event as follows:

I would have to look back in time to see when but my sense is...it (the above dreamwork) was important in my detachment from my husband ...a process of defining myself almost for the first time in my life otherwise I always have been in a relationship...and I am now already in a process of clarification ...of stocktaking... standing back...as to what is me and what is him...and if on my own what is me...what would I do ? who am I? if I was on my own how would I do...it is not clear if I am in a relationship all the time...I'm not sure who is supporting who...when I seem to need to know who I am and what I might be capable of and that suddenly became part of my agenda and that dream and the way I worked on it...it was very powerful...I think it had an energising effect on that process and I couldn't ignore any more that my husband was in the hearse and in mourning (morning) suit...I could have put it to one side if I hadn't worked on it...but because I had made it public and worked on it and involved others in it...it had consolidated its importance.

*The importance of that time was making a public declaration that I didn't love my husband? think that was correct...**the dream gave me a vehicle to say that**...I had said that to myself but not in public.*

X. did that influence your life? *I told him eventually.*

This second example particularly shows how emotionally unexpected and indeed emotionally disturbing the contents of a gestalt exercise can be. Although the dreamer had some 'secret' insight into her present feelings for her husband she had not shared them publicly, and this act of definition to others, generated change in herself and her relationship with her husband. As she said in the interview, *it was very powerful.. it had an energising effect on that process and I couldn't ignore anymore that* my husband *was in the hearse and in morning/mourning suit.* The dream gave her then a **vehicle to say that** and the pun on the word vehicle is I think unintentional! The 'secret' knowledge of the body as Bourdieu (1977) uses that notion is triggered into consciousness by the gestalt exercise and the reflective process on the dream. Whilst the manifest content of the dream is quite clear in so far as the image of her husband is precise, the context of her husband as 'being dead' yet paradoxically dressed as for his marriage brings into play a crucial contradiction of marriage and death in one and the same scenario. The dreamer is almost forced by the dream and the ensuing gestalt exercise to confront the paradoxical imagery and delve into whatever existential meaning they might hold for her. That meaning is her current emotional response to her husband and her view on the original act of marriage itself. Moreover 'being the hearse/car' is an active identification with a dream symbol that confronts her with unexpectedly positive imagery of herself as, *quite flashy..cutting a good figure.* The affirmation of self present in this part of the session is in contrast to the deeply sad and tearful expression of feelings when she is dialoguing (talking) with the 'dead husband'. Also 'being the car' allows her to change the imaginative situation and develop her feeling response as she does. She allows the 'dead body' in the hearse to slip out, and experiences the relief of being unencumbered with it. This imaginative letting go of the image of her dead husband in his marriage suit enables her to dialogue with him and so confront her own present feeling state. Particularly, the gestalt process allows the dreamer to construct an acceptable account of her domestic predicament both to herself and others. This gestalt exercise then again illustrates the process of the generation of meaning both to self and others. The final gestalt example I offer is a form of group gestalt. The dream was a recurrent dream:

people were actually destroying my luggage that I had piled into a van...I was getting ready to start...I was in the house...I was really furious with people...picked up and threw a telephone at them through two windows and a room...the wires got entangled and the house caught fire and was collapsing around me...I got outside...got luggage onto a van...people were firing...they were shooting at the van...I was trying to shield myself...I run towards another door then suddenly I found myself holding a few months old child...but the baby is able to articulate a whole sentence which I wrote down in the dream but I don't remember it.

72

In this section I want to show how the group members imaginatively identified with the 'child image' in the dream and then, from that position, gave a response to the dreamer. The dream involved the man trying to start a journey, throwing a telephone, a house catching fire, people shooting at him...holding a few months old baby. X is the dreamer:

F. *I want to give you a message about that baby...when you were talking about the baby I had a powerful connection about it...it is very hard to say...but I am the baby and I am love and I am open...also take me with you.*

G. *The feeling I had was that if I were the baby and you want to desperately protect me...the message is that I am a tough baby and I don't need so much mollycoddling as you think I need.*

P. *That is interesting and is in direct contrast to the feeling I had which was 'protect me...nurture me...that is what I need'.*

Q. *I have a feeling of peace and strength around the baby...thinking of Christ as a baby asleep in the storm in the boat...as this baby I want to say I feel safe with you...you will look after me.*

H. *I feel the same...I know you are already cherishing me and thank you.*

J. *You protect the baby instinctively even though bullets are flying...the baby wants to make the changes...the baby wants to come out...baby message is 'get me out of the closet'.*

T. *I catch something like that the baby is saying it doesn't matter that you haven't a particular message as the message is 'trust the wisdom of the child'.*

X. *Thank you.*

I. *The brightness and sunshine of the child struck me in contrast to the darkness and the fear...like a pool of light in the dark...an interesting symbol to meditate on.*

Y. *It is something to do with a new beginning...a new opportunity ...amidst all the chaos is the seed.*

X. *That is nice as I feel just absolute chaos and turmoil inside of me... nice thought that there is a still focused part.*

F. *I feel it is not just an ordinary baby but one with a voice with skills way beyond its years...a very special quality.*

O. *This may be facetious now you have no phone there is no-one to intrude...phones are a terrible thing and now you can relate without the phone interrupting.*

X. *That is an interesting thought...Thank you very much everyone...that is very helpful as the child is the one thing I couldn't understand as it was an absolute puzzle and it does fit in with what I need to do in my life.*

This exercise involved each group member giving the dreamer the message that they imagined the child would have given. As can be seen the messages given are contradictory. Interestingly a male member says *'I am a*

tough baby and I don't need so much mollycoddling as you think', whereas
female members stress the nurturing and caring needs of the baby. The
result of this exercise is best expressed in the dreamer's own words later in
the individual interview:

*It was about nurturing the child in me...maybe about mourning my lost
childhood and nurturing the child in me...I have been doing
transactional analysis (note 2)...recently I easily slip over into either my
frightened child or angry parent in terms of my emotional
reactions...hence this conflict as to what I do with my needy child...this
has undone part of the value of this dreamwork through my needing to
nurture this child and then I feel one of my problems is that I get into this
needy child syndrome...maybe I am in touch too much...the dream made
me feel I was okay...a lot of my adult life has been about proving myself
and getting acceptance such as by qualifications and travelling and
living abroad and becoming an X...you can be accepted as a child...
accepted as being rather than as doing...that insight is important and I
bring it with me into this situation...for instance working on the dream
allowed me to relax and to say to myself get on with what I was doing...it
legitimised and authenticated my choices...the dream was a milestone in
terms of my life...rather than something coming out of it...my life was
taking shape...I was doing things with my life..I got a lot of insight from
the dream and the work gave me an insight and took away the fear and
gave me a feeling of acceptance.*

The interview statement is clear as to the value of 'working' on the dream
and also the child image. The dreamer identifies the 'child' image with his
lost intuitive self, that he has now made sacrifices for, in order to reclaim
this part of himself and so seek 'wholeness'. Overall the gestalt exercises
analysed here and also those described elsewhere allow the dreamer, with
facilitation, to identify with the dream symbol and experience in the 'here
and now' the potential multiple referents of that symbol. How much there is
invention and projection onto the symbol, particularly in the group gestalt
case, remains an open question. However the transcripts do show the
creation of meaning in action. The process of association and identification
of meaning with the dream symbolism is the crux of the dreamwork.
Gestalt practices are particularly effective at evoking buried insights and
emotions of the self and in so doing leading to new formulations, and
anticipations of resolutions of core human dilemmas. Moreover during
gestalt exercises in dreamwork, the sense of self is expanded to include an
imaginative identification with all parts of the dream. In the exercises the
dreamer/narrator 'acts as if' they are the 'bread', the 'sherry glass', their
mother etc. This reformulation of the self can be powerful in reshaping the
boundaries of consciousness.
    Gestalt then is a technique of 'self-construction' as Jedrej and Shaw
(1993, p.14), drawing on Foucault's concept, observe in their recent review

of anthropological studies of the cultural role and construction of the social meaning of dream use in contemporary and traditional African societies. Gestalt, and the other experiential techniques presented in this book, allow a playing with the self through which the personal and social identity of the narrator is invented, rehearsed and sometimes affirmed and legitimised through the group process. This invention of self occurs through the interplay of both the ontological and cultural aspects of the self. Dreams manifest the available ontology of the self in a multitude of colourful symbolic forms which are already potentially charged with implicit and embodied personal and cultural meanings. These symbolic forms suggest original pathways towards identity construction previously unknown by the person. The car as we saw becomes a hearse, an escort, and also a 'cutting figure' through which the dreamer/narrator can explore hidden meanings using the cultural symbolism of cars in modern society. The remembered and dreamt metaphor becomes a living metaphor for the narrator and for the group. The construction of meaning is fused with the performance of social action. Meaning, social action and power intersect as Jedrej and Shaw argue (1993, p.8). Moreover the self is acted upon by the group as well as in the private fantasy world of the individual. Such a re-identification of the self is not without personal and even cultural consequences. In particular the group gestalt exercise on the 'baby' symbol, which has just been described, allowed the entire group to imaginatively identify with the dreamt and narrated images. In this sense gestalt exercises involve the transformation of a remembered visual image into a metaphorical summary of core attributes of the self or, as I have defined this result, into a 'mini-archetype'. Such a process also would occur using psychodrama as a process.

Psychodrama and sculpting

Psychodrama is a kind of role-play or re-enactment of some past or possibly future situation. Such a dramatic re-creation of past or possible events is a group-based activity initiated in the 1920s by Moreno (Brazier,1991, p.2). In the drama the group members are used to act the different roles of a particular situation concerning one of their members. Since a 'typical' psychodrama evokes strong emotion concerning basic human experiences like loss, love and fear, the feelings of the rest of the members of the group will be evoked. Facilitating respondents to do a psychodrama in a therapeutic situation may allow the respondents to rehearse and often to experience a form of catharsis about an unfinished aspect of their own personal lives. Such a process of involvement may, and often does, generate new insight and reformulation of the concept of self. In a different way the experience for respondents of considering how their dream image might relate to their present situation may, on occasions, generate a fresh perspective on their personal and social preoccupations and on those of others involved.

In a psychodrama the director negotiates the development of the drama with the subject of the drama, the protagonist. The protagonist describes the interpersonal situation they want to work on and gives information to the group about the participants in that situation. The protagonist chooses from the group, people s/he wants to represent the identified people in the situation. If it is a family situation s/he may choose parents, a grandparent, siblings and their own children, partner etc. After the actors have received sufficient information to dramatise the story the psychodrama or enactment takes place with the director checking its authenticity with the protagonist who usually plays themself to begin with. Thereafter the drama can be developed in any imaginative form. The protagonist can take over being a parent or a sibling, for instance, and speak and act from that position. If a new character is referred to, perhaps an aunt, the play can shift to enacting an imaginary scene between the protagonist, the aunt and whoever. The 'dead' can come back to life and the living can speak to the 'dead'.

Sculpting involves a group member using some of the other group members physically to represent past or present relationships in the former's current family, family of origin, or a significant group such as a work group. The person doing the sculpt arranges the key people to display how he or she feels or would like to represent the group or family in question. So a sculpt may display the whole gamut of feelings in relationships whether they be togetherness, security, conflict, anger or hurt. Alliances and hostilities in a group can easily be shown by using typical motifs such as 'the clenched fist' or 'hugging', and the spatial representation of people through closeness and distance is a powerful way to express feelings. The 'sculptor' may be very surprised by how he places significant people in his/her life, such as siblings or parents. The 'knowledge' that he/she represents in the sculpt may be surprising, and may show feelings and perceptions that have until this point remained unacknowledged. The evocation of such unacknowledged perceptions through the use of techniques such as sculpting and psychodrama, if utilised by a researcher, would allow them the opportunity to access significantly deeper perceptions than an interview or questionnaire normally allows. Perceptions of which the respondent is barely conscious can then become conscious.

Psychodrama is a powerful form of working and small scale dramatisations were quite often done in the dreamwork groups. For instance there was the re-enactment of the situation of the dreamer asserting herself towards the harassing young boys, described in the previous section on gestalt methods. Only on one occasion was a larger dramatisation implemented. This was based on a drama of the female dreamer holding a baby in an apartment in New York where two rats attack the baby. The rat is killed by the dreamer who later throws away the baby. This is a brief report of the dream whose enactment principally involved the rats attacking the baby and the later dialoguing between the mother and the baby.

However, whilst the drama was vivid and engaging there is little evidence that insight was generated or at least made explicit to the group. Sculpting was not used but is reported in Cushway and Sewell's work (1992, p.68).

Imagework

Imagework has developed from the active imagination technique of Jung and the theory and practice of psychosynthesis developed by Assagioli (1965, p.11-34). More recently transpersonal psychotherapy has integrated the work of Assagioli and Jung to form an imaginatively based approach to therapy. Rowan says that:

> In active imagination we fix upon a particular point, mood, picture or event, and then allow a fantasy to develop in which certain images become concrete or even personified. Thereafter the images have a life of their own and develop according to their own logic (1993, p.51).

This is an active process in which the person actively imagining 'lets go' of the mind's normal train of thoughts and images and goes with a sequence of imagery that arises spontaneously from the unconscious. It is this quality of spontaneity and unexpectedness that are the hallmarks of this process. A very typical exercise of this type is for the facilitator of the exercise, after an introductory relaxation exercise, to lead the participants on a journey. A classical form of this is to start the journey in a meadow and to lead participants over an obstacle and up a hill to a house on the hill where they meet a wise person who they can talk to about any question that they have. An exercise like this is described in Ernst and Goodison (1981, p.161) and, in my experience can trigger disclosure of and work on important personal issues. Examples I have encountered in leading such sessions are those where either participants deal with unresolved grief issues or they rehearse the outcomes of possible important decisions. Moreover the quality and characteristics of the environment in such a fantasy journey are seen by practitioners as indicating aspects of an individual's personal state. To Ernst and Goodison, many features encountered in such a journey, even the weather, may indicate the individual's present feeling state, whether of happiness or of sadness. Likewise the type and difficulty of the obstacle met and the method of overcoming it may indicate the current level and development of problem-solving skills.

Imagework exercises that I led in the groups were based on motifs or images that developed spontaneously from group members' dreams. Such examples of imagework are a member's 'being a plant bulb' in their imagination; another 'being a bird' and finally 'going through a door' in the mind. In the last case two group members had coincidentally dreamt of not going through a door during a recent dream. I will now show by means of an example the impact and value of using this approach as a research as well

a personal growth technique. In the example the guided fantasy was based
on the dream of a member which she had worked on during the session. In
the dream she had dreamt of a vast beautiful brown bird with a very large
wing span. During the dream sequence the bird had become split into two
layers and one half had flown off. This had been experienced as a powerful
dream image, both by the group and by the dreamer. Two weeks later
another group member dreamt about her son, and about her being about to
fly off with him, using some lively leather wings. The initial discussion and
sharing of recent dreams that week seemed to include lots of reference to
travelling. Another mentioned that all her recent dreams had been about
travelling. We decided then to do a guided fantasy to explore this theme of
travel in the group. I led this fantasy journey. Following a relaxation
exercise, I suggested that members could become any bird they liked and
then I followed on with a set of spontaneous travel instructions with long
intervals in between my speaking in order to allow members to go where
they wished. Probably the fantasy lasted about twenty minutes in total and
on this occasion had not been prepared, but had developed 'spontaneously'
out of the themes and imagery around in the group. The range of
experiences people have during these exercises is very wide. One member
became an owl and couldn't get going until they had found (imagined) a
puffin to go with; another was a bird in the Andes mountain range; another
was a swallow and flew off to Capri; another a soft brown bird sitting in a
tree; another a brown gull going to Portugal; another became a Canadian
Goose and migrated down the West coast of the United Stated of America.
    The example I will now consider involves another member who in this
fantasy journey became a parakeet bird and flew over the jungle. The
following is their description of their fantasy journey transcribed from a
tape recording of the session following the fantasy exercise. The member
had been too disturbed by their experience to share it at the end of the actual
exercise:

> Basically I was a parakeet...I lived in a garden in Sydney Australia
> ...together with a great many of my family...and I was flying in response
> to instructions to go a long distance...I flew to the coast...a tropical
> region and then it was a bit drastic...I disintegrated and my integrity
> could not be retained...and I became...I spread out as bits and pieces of
> head feathers claw etc over a jungle and I became a jungle and then of
> course I could not come back and at that point I decided I could not cope
> with this and I went quite deep inside and surfaced again later...I took all
> that home with me and by the time I had finished looking at it I had
> become happy being a jungle and felt very much at home as that there
> ...but I was totally unable to follow instructions...I was a disobedient
> bird!

The member concerned said that she had 'got a lot out of' the exercise but
had been disturbed by the experience. Another member suggested to the

first member that she had found 'her place' and the first member thoughtfully said 'yes'. That was the extent of the disclosure during that session. Several months later I interviewed her. In the intervening period the member had shared to the group that she had decided to finish her marriage and had negotiated a separation from her husband. She had become much more open and expressive in the group and according to herself she was living her life much more authentically in general. The following quote is from her description and reflection on the exercise several months later in the interview.

I ask this member about how she had understood this guided fantasy and she said, *I have arrived in the Jungle and I am very pleased to be here and it is just amazing!* I asked her about the connection she now made between herself and the jungle image and, after describing how horrendous the experience had been she said:

> *I exploded...I wiped myself out but it was meant to be like that...*and going on she spoke about the, *jungle entity itself...all sorts of different components...all growing and moving...nurturing each other...tangled... full of unseen but not necessarily dangerous...but it was an exciting environment ...It was full of sound and potential...full of growth...It was precarious possibly but I don't myself feel precarious.*

I asked if that description of the jungle reflected how she now felt about her life and she emphatically said, *yes,* and that she felt, *she had shed a lump of concrete and had great energy levels now.* This sequence shows that whilst, in this example, the image sequence experienced had been frightening at the time, the dreamer had reflected upon it and had come to see how the experience of being suddenly transformed from a small bird in a family of birds into a jungle represented metaphorically her own transformation from being married for many years into being in a separated state. The frightening image of the jungle had become a very positive image for her. The example from this piece of imagework shows imaginatively the time and nature of a transition in the person's social state, personal identity, capacity to change and ability to conceptualise the self.

The second example of imagework is from the third guided fantasy in which members had to imagine themselves designing a door in their minds and then going through it. The idea for this exercise came after, coincidentally, two members talked of dreaming of locked doors. The exercise started with an instruction to go down an escalator and there find a guide and a 'magic carpet'. The most substantial fantasy reported after this exercise was the following one:

> *There was a lovely rich Turkish guide there...I had to leave him behind...then I got to the door very quickly and there was a flight of steps...of dark grey steps...I had been given a little golden key...I put it round my neck...I was waiting for instructions to open the door...I was*

79

*then in a vast soaring cathedral with vast arches...it was quite
dim....suddenly it becomes lighter in the cathedral...the stone around is
warmer honey-coloured not grey and the door becomes lighter in
texture...then all these people there come pouring in from every direction
and I went into the cathedral again...the first impression was light and
colour and richness...like in the Orthodox churches the eye is drawn up
to these cavernous spaces and I had the impression of light coming in
from up there...I floated up into the air and I was drawn up there...I
thought I was going to be shown something in this place...it was very
much built like a mandala in the centre...there was no altar but rather a
centre piece...the centre piece was a gold cross and I wasn't sure what I
was meant to be doing with all these people...so I asked my guide to
come...I was reluctant to face them at first...here was a gold dish with
circular wafers on...not like the church tradition I was brought up
in...and I felt resistant to that and to taking a wafer and I missed that out
and went back to it later and I had to stand in the centre...and I was
given a tiny little...I am mixed up...when I was up there I looked down at
the centre and was given a gold chalice with wine in it and then I had to
go down there and drink the wine...and I had a wafer and then I had
done that...there was loads of bread...lovely warm granary rolls and I
was giving everyone there it and I told them to sit down...and my guide
put a robe round my shoulders and told me to dance and then I danced
and the tune that came to me was the 'lord of the dance' and I danced out
of the door and all the people came out and it was a hillside now outside
the church and they went off happy with their bread and I didn't want to
get back on the carpet and I walked down the hillside and I lay on my
blanket and I had a pillow to sleep on...I needed space after all the
people.*

The discussion after this reporting of the fantasy journey focused on a
career discussion and whether the imagery of the fantasy seemed to be
beckoning the member in some future direction. A substantial discussion as
to the opportunities and the problems with such a decision ensued. The
visualiser spoke of how it was the first time for years that she:

> *hadn't been doing some kind of...X activity...I have been lying fallow...
> things don't seem to be happening in the right direction...I have been
> feeling all day how much pain in the world there is...have had a bad time
> at work recently...the whole world has been crying out...but they* (the
> people in the fantasy) *went away happily.*

The dreamer fits the experience of this imagery and the later discussion
into daytime categorisations which are seen as representing an optimistic
expression of her inclination to make a particular career choice in the future,
whatever the obstacles. This she did attempt to do.

Artwork

Artwork is often used as one method of working with dreams and images. Group members are offered the opportunity to draw their sequence of mental imagery of the dream they have had. In this way they objectify the imagery and offer themselves the opportunity to relate to the imagery outside themselves as well as providing a way in for others to share insights, make suggestions and otherwise dialogue with the now externalised imagery. Benson has written about the use of artwork that:

> These techniques emphasise the feeling and intuitive aspects of personality and offer a valuable way of exploring events in the group life which are not always logical or are hard to talk about in a coherent way (1987, p.213).

Again we see the possible benefits of using these approaches to reveal and disclose those things which the respondent is either most anxiously concealing, or has already concealed from themselves. Although art materials were available every week in the second and third dreamwork groups they were only used on one occasion. However because the artwork was actually done in pairs, the ensuing dialogue was also in pairs and was therefore not available for analysis.

Meditation and dream re-entry

Meditative technique was only used once in the groupwork process. This involved a relaxation exercise, the opportunity to choose a previous 'good' experience in life, and finally the introduction of this developed meditative state into a recent dream experience. The meditation went as follows:

> *Go into your inner space...relax your body and be open...let your body relax ...become aware of the breath...become aware of preoccupations and as you breathe think how you want to deal with the preoccupations ...breathe them out...spend two to three minutes letting go of those preoccupations...go back to a time in life when you felt very centred and very true to yourself...try to recall in detail what is going on in your life...what is happening...what are you doing...how are you behaving ...how does it feel to be behaving in this way...being really true to yourself...what image or sound or colour can you associate with being centred?...let one come to you...in your imagination take yourself into a dream that you have talked about tonight...what does that dream want of*

you? how does it reveal your true self?...come back to an awareness of the group with the awareness you have found.

Group members experienced this meditation, led by my colleague, as very positive and commented as such in the individual interviews. The following are two examples of the experiences people reported after this meditation:

> *I remembered being on a marathon course in Amsterdam...felt very energised at 4.00 in morning and everyone was flagging and I got everyone dancing and I was dressed in golden white clothes and I took this image into the dream and I took the golden me into the dream and took the me that was in the dream and was the rejected one and I took the other two and we made a circle around her and she was in the middle and she was brown and X. was blue and the party girl was there and she was red and I was golden...then I brought the other people from the party in and they made two circles round us outside and then everybody put one hand on the person in front and one hand on the person on the side of them and it was like a healing web...I feel quite choked about the woman being in the middle.*

This example of a narrated dream re-entry relates to a 'jealousy' dream in which the dreamer sees her male partner intimately dancing with another woman. The meditation exercise involves a dream re-entry stage in which the 'good' sense of self evoked by the meditation is 'taken into' the dream. This 'good' sense of herself is represented by her as being dressed in 'golden white clothes'. As this 'other' self the dreamer is able to 'redraw' the dream imagery and reach a more acceptable conclusion to what we saw had been a very distressing event. The dreamer 'draws' two circles of people around the dancing couple, which includes her partner, who has made her feel jealous in the original dream. All the people in the circles touch each other making for the dreamer a kind of 'healing web'. This 'healing web' probably refers to a refiguration of emotion in herself in relation to her previous emotional experience of the dream imagery. She can be seen as regaining power in the imaginative situation by redrawing and completing the sequence of imagery in a way more acceptable to herself. In this the notion of 'more acceptable' seems to reflect a public encircling and containment of the dangerous pair. The next example of feedback from the meditative exercise refers to the following dream and its immediate discussion. X is the dreamer:

> X. *I was on an escalator...I was with my flatmate and I was very angry with her...here were things that I really had wanted to say to her for a long time and she was just saying yes yes and that is all.*
>
> *I . What things exactly?*

*X. Things like I am not putting up with this any more...I have had enough
of it and I am moving out and I am not just here for your defensive
and aggressive statements...she was wearing a hat.*

I . Is that how you were feeling?

*X. It was...we were very good friends and we moved in together...but this
was not a good idea...I have lots of annoying habits...it is better now
but still there are irritating aspects.*

Her feedback from the meditation and dream re-entry was as follows:

It feels really good (about the meditation and centering image)...*I was on
the escalator in bathing shorts and it was hot and I felt so free...saying I
am free and I can do what I want...I haven't thought back to that time
and I feel really good to be that sort of person.*

In the individual interview the dreamer referred to this experience in the
following way:

*In the dream about my flatmate on the escalator...it was about getting
anger off my chest...it was a really good experience to have worked on in
the meditation...in the meditation you could do what you really
wanted...in the dream I then felt fantastic as I realised I didn't have to
take on all this stuff...the dream reflected real life...the dreamwork really
affected my behaviour as I changed my behaviour...I found I was being
too accommodating to avoid conflict with my housemate...it was really
good...in the meditation you had to take out a word and I took out 'free'
and I realised I had not had this...realised I could change...I felt
empowered to change.*

The above example shows well the change effect of the meditative
process and dream re-entry and subsequent discussion. The dreamwork
during the session has evoked a connection for the dreamer between the
dream imagery and her present anger and frustration with her flatmate. The
meditation evokes a strong self-perception that allows her to feel in control
of the situation through decision and anticipated future action. The dreamer
describes this process later as 'feeling empowered'. She feels she has gained
power within her domestic situation through the whole dreamwork process.
Buried feelings have been actively related to her perception of her
relationship with her flatmate, and at the same time her manner of coping
with her present situation reflects her understanding of her personality
patterns, and their strengths and weaknesses.

The methods described in this chapter show a range of applications of
creative action-based groupwork techniques derived often from the
humanistic groupwork tradition. They range from the less to the more
complicated. Discussion and personal contextualisation is the articulation
of a straightforward process. The use of some of the techniques of gestalt

and psychodrama, as outlined in this chapter, do not need lengthy training, but rather a willingness to experiment within a structured and safe group environment. Advanced training in these methods is however available. Artwork, meditation and imagework can be used sensitively again without extensive training. The next chapter analyses the importance of the group context and group process for an understanding and practice of dreamwork.

Notes

1. 'Doubling' is the action in psychodrama when one or more of the group, not the protagonist or director, go behind the protagonist and imaginatively speak as they feel the protagonist is 'really' feeling and thinking. There can also be one 'double' with the protagonist throughout the psychodrama.

2. 'Transactional Analysis' is a psychotherapeutic approach developed by Eric Berne (1964) and involves an application of game theory to interpersonal situations. It is also a conceptualisation and analysis of the self as being constituted primarily by three core aspects of: parent, adult and child.

6 The group context

This chapter focuses on the group, its dynamic process and how this process interacted with the dreamwork. In particular I consider the following: characteristics of the members; the stages of the group; decision-making and leadership; conflict and communication; the development of group identity; trust and self-disclosure; members' evaluation of the group. Overall this chapter analyses the dynamic and interactive aspects of the group's life. Tedlock's communicative theory of dreaming proposes that such an analysis of the social dynamics of the dream sharing be considered as an essential aspect of any anthropology of dreaming and also provides a theoretical and applied framework for understanding dreamwork within Western culture.

Membership (see appendix for table of members' backgrounds)

The composition of the groups' membership has already been substantially described in the introduction so as to provide a basis for the reader to understand the ongoing references to the group case-studies. The following is additional information about the characteristics of group membership. Several members knew one or more group members prior to joining the group and this prior knowledge was a significant dynamic on occasions within the group. For instance, on one occasion when discussing a dream image about 'laying paving stones', a member reminded the dreamer that they had given her advice when laying out the garden in her present house. Occasionally prejudices about one another appeared to come to the fore in, for example, whether to interpret a dream image sexually or not. Access to 'privileged' and prior knowledge of the dreamer was claimed by another member on at least one occasion. Some members knew each other from circle dancing and this provided a familiarity for some new members. There was a variety of attitudes to the value of dreaming. Many members thought dream imagery was in some way potentially relevant and useful for their waking lives, but felt that a pondering alone on the meaning of their imagery was necessarily limited. Others were coming to the group primarily for its potentially supportive role and for a 'space' in which they could share their current concerns. One group member who articulated this perspective particularly strongly stated that the dreamwork part of the group was incidental to her and she felt that dreams were vehicles to represent and share intimate life concerns. She spoke also of the 'undefended self' encountered in dreamwork. Another member said he was coming to the group to gain experience of groupwork and had little awareness of his own dreams. Another who attended most of the second group believed strongly that all dreams were prophetic and came from a strong 'religious' or at least 'spiritualistic' background.

Stages of the groups

A common feature of theorising about groupwork (Benson,1987 p.84; Brown,1979, p.66; Preston-Shoot,1987, p.111) is a concern with the issue of the group process as exhibiting various stages. These theorists present groups as typically passing through common stages. Tuckman (1965, pp.384-99) describes these as 'forming, storming, norming and performing', whilst Schutz (1979, pp.11-137) describes a developmental pattern involving stages described as inclusion, control and affection. The value of such formulations is the idea of some kind of potential pattern to the mosaic of possible group events and processes. At the beginning of their existence groups typically are concerned with issues of emotional belonging, of whether the individual members 'feel' or expect to 'feel' comfortable and accepted within the group. Members typically experience ambivalence at this stage as to whether the group is 'right' for them. Anxiety, whether manifest as silence or loquaciousness, is a typical feature of this stage. After the issue of belonging has begun to be resolved, the group begins to focus on its perceived task and deals with power issues between members and with the group leaders. This is usually called the 'storming' stage and as this metaphor suggests this is a typical time of conflict and rivalry, about, for instance, the actual aims of the group and interpersonal power. However it is important to realise that such group stages do not occur in a standard linear pattern but rather the stages snake in and out, and events and developments within and sometimes outside the group can precipitate 'storming' sequences. As I will show later the three dreamwork groups encountered and developed different conflicts and issues in their time. In the linear pattern I am (with some reservation) outlining, groups, having navigated the stage of critical and political definition, can then embark on their actual work. In this case it was the discussion of dreams and the search for meaning within and through the discussion of dreams. In all three groups this stage was reached and 'the work' of the group was achieved. The groups 'formed' into an effective form and pattern for their task, and this effective form tends to be considered as a set of norms. In groupwork literature 'performing' is often the final stage of the groupwork process and defines the period in the group when the work of the group moves forward without time being absorbed in, for instance, defining the task and the roles of the members. The stage of 'norming' tends to blur into that of 'performing' and generally refers to a satisfactory group climate in which members are contributing well and where there is a high and developing degree of trust and coherence. I will outline the development of the three groups giving examples of these stages.

First group

This was a small group with only six members. It developed very quickly and was characterised by a high degree of experimentation in ways of working with dreams. It was in this group that methods such as gestalt, psychodrama, meditation, fantasy work were used for the first time. The group rapidly developed a high level of trust and coherence and quickly developed norms that lasted throughout all the three groups. For instance the practice of 'doing a round' at the beginning to allow members to share how they were feeling in the present was adopted. This beginning with a 'round' is a typical groupwork device and has several functions: among them are the equalisation of speaking roles, the opportunity to impart critical personal information to the group and the opportunity to 'leave aside' current preoccupations and to focus on the group session. As part of these rounds we established that members should briefly share if they had a dream or not and the present value and intensity of that dream. This member evaluation of their dream helped establish whether the dream was short or long; powerful or not; single or recurrent. This disclosure allowed the group and its facilitators to begin to prioritise which dreams to 'work on'. The group then rapidly established itself as an entity with agreements about when and how often to meet. Rules of confidentiality and agreement about tape-recording were discussed and agreed. The session began with the lighting of candles in a candelabra and burning an incense stick and finished with the candles being blown out. Refreshments were taken at the end of the first two groups and during a mid-meeting break in the third group. This first group quickly developed a cohesion and a commitment to experiment. In the second week the group did a guided fantasy based on the image of a flower bulb which had been described as part of a dream worked on during the first week. Members also had the opportunity, during this guided fantasy, to remember any dreams they had had and to symbolise these in terms of an image or object. Then they, metaphorically speaking, brought these back to the group, like a souvenir from a journey. The variety of symbols and images coming back ranged from a gold chalice, a silver cup, a picture of stones under swift flowing water, an eagle and an image of being burnt at a stake! These disclosures to the group and the discussions provoked by them facilitated a rapid coming together of group members and a sense of excitement as to the potentiality of the group. In fact, towards the end of the first group one member commented ironically that 'we' knew much about the unconscious lives of group participants but surprisingly little about their daytime identities and preoccupations. In the final session of the life of this first group no dreams were discussed. Instead one member discussed a pressing relationship issue and received supportive feedback from the group members. This ability of the group to suspend 'dreamwork' on occasion was to be a feature of all three groups and it occurred in approximately one session during each ten session period.

Different group members experienced the group process differently. In interview one member said in response to the question 'What did the group mean to you?'

I felt really ignorant in relation to the group especially at first...One day I went away feeling really awful...On the third week I felt bad through not contributing enough...it felt difficult to speak my mind about dreams in the group...I felt I was letting others do the work...I nearly didn't go back then but the next week it was brilliant...I worked on a dream and then we did a guided fantasy/meditation with one of the facilitators...I was able to really understand the dream...then I really started to enjoy the sessions and then I couldn't go to the last two sessions...I gained confidence...I don't have to feel inferior.

Second group

This began several weeks after the first one ended and after the Christmas break. The break was longer than usual to allow for one group member to return from a long holiday and so rejoin the group at the beginning. The second group contained twelve members and was probably too large for a dreamwork group. All the members from the first group except one returned to the second group. There was surprisingly little friction between 'old' and 'new' members and this ease was probably caused by the characters of the new members, who were energetic and ready to 'work' and share dreams from the outset of the group. Moreover, as already indicated, some 'new' members were either already friends or knew some 'old' members. Moreover the group soon began to enter into a conflictual area in relation to the 'different' orientation of one of the 'new' group members. Whilst this issue will be developed in the next section on 'conflict', the group's focus on resulting interpersonal and leadership issues seriously affected the group's ability either to 'norm' or 'perform', to use that terminology of group process. The effective departure of that member towards the end of the second group's life allowed the group to 'do' some dreamwork and some discussion of dreams occurred in every session. However the impact of the interpersonal difficulty, differences expressed as to orientation towards dreamwork and the meaning of the dreams had significantly impeded the development of group trust and group coherence. One male group member reflecting on the experience of the two groups said:

..the first group was the most exciting time...we worked together really well...conflicts got resolved...I experienced a very positive lot of action...In the second group I was grateful that the group start was delayed as there was a lot going on in my life...It was a bigger group of people who I didn't know...the group went down...I got quite stuck in it and things didn't get resolved as in the first group...there was a lot of unfinished business...which was resolved by the two most prickly members leaving the group...they were potentially very valuable members.

Third group

The composition of the third group was different from the first two. Three new members joined and three members from the second group left. Two of the three 'new' members left after one week, apparently because they, certainly one of them, had wanted a more directive group. The third 'new' member left after three sessions for reasons he reported as *'wanting more challenge in the group'*. However the 'old' members recognised that due to the prior cohesion of the group, the third group was probably a difficult group for 'new' members to join without feeling excluded. This left a group of nine members, of whom one didn't come towards the end of the sequence. The group ran for nine weeks and finished with a party on the tenth week to which almost all members who had been at the three groups were invited and came. The time of the weekly sessions in this third group was extended to two and a half hours instead of two hours though often in this sequence there was a refreshment break in the middle of the session.

This third group was characterised by several features. Firstly the dynamic innovation of the first group was somewhat absent with less innovative groupwork practice and more reliance on simple discussion of dreams. Secondly, there was again a high level of trust and group coherence established and particularly high levels of self-disclosure were manifest in this group. In the middle of the sequence, there was a noteworthy session in which coincidentally three female members disclosed either that they were in the process of leaving their long term male partners or were effectively considering this. No discussion of dreams again took place in that session but as a consequence there was a resulting focus on women members disclosing personal issues and some criticism of male members for their reluctance or inability to conceptualise and communicate about their emotional lives in a group setting. The group during this period was described as 'being like a women's group'. For instance in the sixth session the focus of the group discussion was on why and when women leave long term relationships and the resulting costs and dilemmas concerning money and children that result. This emphasis on greater female participation in the group and a feminisation of group issues was a feature for the second half of the third group. Male members were not excluded, but at least one felt pressed into sharing more intimate aspects of himself with the group than he felt at ease with. At the beginning of the session after the partnership disclosures, he said that he had felt 'pressed to speak' and had felt uncomfortable because of this. He further felt that he had had to carry 'guilt as a male' but had realised that the issues being discussed were his also.

Overall the three groups had different characteristics due to changing membership structures. For those members who were present throughout the three groups, the three separate groups probably felt more like three separate stages of the same group, there being a core of members throughout the three groups.

Group norms

In the previous section on stages of the life of groups, reference has already been made to the development of group norms as being indicative of group development. Norms quickly became established about how the group should spend its time. Smith states, with reference to his review of the study of group norms that the following norms would typically be approved by most members in encounter-type groupwork settings:

> .... all groups approved of asking for feedback, talking about the here and now, giving feedback, challenging the leader, and probing a member who had been silent. Virtually all groups disapproved of putting down a member who had just opened up with personal feelings, talking a lot without showing one's real feelings, and being frequently absent from the group (1980, pp.19-20).

In the first session a balance between action work, in this case a gestalt exercise, and discussion on the dream narrative took place. This set a pattern for subsequent sessions. Most weeks one or more of the following methods such as gestalt, psychodrama, guided fantasy or meditation was used to facilitate the dreamwork. Every dream 'worked on' was of course discussed usually beginning with questions of clarification about the dream imagery and its narration such as 'was there anyone else in the room?' or 'what colour were the clothes you were wearing?' Whilst the group and its facilitators were ideologically firmly set against interpreting anyone's dream, there was often a suggestive process. Members might suggest a way of looking at a dream such as, 'Have you explored looking at ....?' or 'Perhaps you are identifying too much with the X role?' By the end of the groups two processes had developed in relation to suggestion. Firstly the boundary around a suggestion was more clearly asserted and so a member intending to make a suggestion would introduce it with the following preamble, 'If that were my dream, I would..... think about it in that way'. This helped to clarify the point that any comments made by a group member to the dream narrator were likely to be personally projective to some extent. A member asserted the importance of members 'owning' their suggestions in the following words:

When you interpret you are saying that here is some useful information about me which I offer you as possibly useful for 'you' therefore it is easier for the dreamworker (narrator) to evaluate interpretations and either accept or reject them.

The further issues around the mode of suggestion by group members has been described in the last chapter. However whilst this apparently exemplary framing of any suggestion was being asserted as the best way to make suggestive comments, the experience for several dream narrators in the group was that they were sometimes bombarded with suggestions that they couldn't assimilate. Criticism was made that members were not always 'respecting the dream' by the multiplicity of suggestion being made. This situation of 'bombardment' was caused by the eagerness of people to share their ideas and projections with the narrator of the dream. The most common method of developing the potential and implicit meaning of a dream for the narrator, after suggestion and clarification, was gestalt identification. As already described, the basic gestalt exercise involved the narrator imaginatively identifying with one part, object or event, from the dream and then describing themselves as if they were that object or event. Further methods of 'working' used were working in pairs and threes on occasions. Usually there was considerable discussion prior to going into any grouping smaller than the large group based on the expressed concern that this would inhibit the development and shared experience of the group. However when this pairs/small group approach was used, approximately once in each ten week sequence, then the results were usually favourable in so far as members could verbally share, or in one case, draw and colour their dream narrative to a greater extent than they could in the large group. The second time when this happened was the occasion involving the faeces dreams, as already mentioned in the 'pair and small groupwork' section in the previous chapter. The development of group norms was not however without areas of conflict emerging and sometimes being resolved.

Group conflict

Conflict is a normal part of group life and can lead onto a resolution or a broader synthesis of aims and means, or it can be destructive for whole or part of the group. Miles says that:

A group without conflict may be in serious difficulty, points of view are being masked and inhibited, and good solutions cannot be worked out (1959, p.25).

91

Douglas (1976, p.117) agrees with this viewpoint, stressing the importance of distinguishing between creative and destructive conflict in a group. Four main areas of conflict emerged in the dreamwork groups studied. These were: the nature of dream interpretation; the nature of the group; the role of myself as facilitator; dealing with the evidently 'different' orientation of one group member. I will discuss each in turn. The key difference concerning interpretation was in relation to the acceptability of a well known part of the Freudian paradigm. There was a split in the group between members who tended to want to interpret dream imagery as covert sexual symbols and those who felt that they were well able to dream explicitly of sexual issues when necessary and resented such sexual interpretations of their imagery. The split between group members on this issue is exemplified by the following dream of a female group member. She dreamt of:

..another woman having a gynaecological operation, lying in a tank of water...One of the doctors was carrying a huge hypodermic syringe and injected it into the women's skull.

The issue of another female group member interpreting this image as a sexual one was still unresolved weeks later when the original dreamer forcefully disclosed to the group that there had been a subsequent and sexually explicit progression in the dream that she had not previously disclosed. The dreamer disclosed this additional information to show to the group that she was able to dream explicitly about sexual matters and to invalidate the suggestion that the hypodermic was a covert sexual symbol. This example also illustrated contemporaneously the importance of non-narration or in this case delayed narration of sensitive dream data.

I have already indicated that members came to the group with different degrees of interest in the study of dreaming itself. At least one member was explicitly seeking a personal support group and felt that dreams provided a suitable vehicle for facilitating discussion about prevalent life concerns. The issue of how much the group was a dreamwork group became manifest only during the middle of the second sequence and was linked to the other conflictual issues relating to my facilitation and the different orientation of one group member. In the sixth week of this group almost the whole session was taken up with the introductory round. This was partly due to substantial feedback from the previous week's experience of a guided fantasy. The frustration felt by some members more interested in doing dreamwork is evident in the following quotation:

K. *I feel a lot of time was spent doing the initial round...losing dreams...it is interesting but!*
Z. *I feel we need time to build up a feeling of safety trust and connection with people before going into the most private space...otherwise I*

would feel most exposed...need trust and confidence to know what to share.

J. *I feel this very strongly...I have a lot of material to share but...I am not happy to share until I have some sense of the other members in the group.*

K. *Time goes very quickly.*

D. *We need to be more brisk.*

H. *We are processing last week this week...we didn't have time last week.*

D. *I am against rigid time slots...it will be different each week.*

F. *It is not a round...it is a to-ing and fro-ing...I am not sure what it is.*

Q. *I need to speak in the first hour get the first two to three sentences out.*

F. *We need structure to do that.*

J. *It feels that it doesn't matter that we are not dreaming much as we are not really working on dreams now...we value other things.*

L. *I want space to hear people's dreams.*

G. *I suggest lengthening the group.*

O. *I feel people wanting varying things in terms of how much structure and space.*

The above discussion illustrates the wide disagreement in the second group at this point. That particular session continued with discussion of the previous week and then moved onto a dream. However in order to try and resolve this situation I started the following week by saying, *'I want the group to do some dreamwork!'*. Shortly afterwards I was confronted by criticism that I had been overdirective:

Z. *I feel upset...I feel I am going to upset the apple cart...I felt uneasy about how the group was started tonight by X. (myself) ...I don't need to be told about dreamwork...to 'get down to business'...I need trust in the facilitator...what is your motivation in starting the group by saying 'let's get going on dreams'...I was one of the first to trust your discretion re recording...last week I began to wonder about that when you spoke about U.*

(Next there is criticism of the way I passed on personal information to this second group. This information was given to me by a group member from the first group who had left at the end of the first group. This information was passed on by me with the member's explicit consent for me to share it with the current group but, due to its importance for other group members following their involvement in that member's psychodrama, I was criticised by Z. for the way in which I had imparted it).

Z. *I was upset* (referring to the imparting of the information) *quite a lot and went away unhappy though I was happy about other parts of the week...I was unhappy about your complete lack of discretion.*

93

I defend myself by saying that:

U. had wanted to communicate this information to the group...and had wanted to say goodbye to the group.
Z. You should have checked out the telling with other members of the group in the psychodrama...I don't want to go back into it as I would have to go back into the dream and recognise difference of perceptions.

I defend my opening remark saying that:

There is a continuum of interest within the group for dreamwork.
K. supported me and said, I was glad to hear news of U. I didn't feel anything had been betrayed.
D. Felt last week was not 'off task'...dreams are a tool to understanding myself...both others and me...we bypassed the dream and got to the real point...the meat of the thing which is the 'undefended self' there was great deal of interaction between them.
F. I agree there is a powerful relationship between my dreams and my life...what we did last week was immensely useful and powerful as a way back into dreams from the bottom rather than the top down.
R. There is a difference in how safe people want to be.
A. Dreams are a way into the undefended self or we can work on dream as a story or picture and therefore the dream is out there and can be worked on quite safely...we can explore the interactive saga of life without a dream and this was happening last week...there are three levels to be worked on...first...straight in like last week...secondly...with the dream out there...thirdly...with the dream as a way into self.
Q. There is too short a time for dreamwork given the amount of time spent on other issues...I think we have got somewhere when we have worked with a dream...you (the facilitators) have set your stall up and I have come to your stall.
J. I feel frustrated about how little time is spent on dreams.
J. Says she has, the 'courage' to talk about a dream.

The dream we then discussed proved to be one of the most valuable both for the individual and the group. The final main area of conflict for the group proved to be the group's response to one member in the second group who demonstrated a markedly different orientation to the dreamwork and who was perceived as having a different way of working in a group. This member disclosed that she had had a history of mental health problems, and arguably, from the perspective of the group, should have been counselled by the facilitators to leave the group. However the facilitators did not do this.

94

In the third session of the second group this member narrated what she called a 'murder dream' which contained very violent imagery and was presented in chapter one. Considerable tension built up in the group following this narration. The narrator ascribed a 'devilish' feel to the dream and monologued about the dream and rejected all attempts by other members to 'work' with the dream imagery in terms of possible linking of the dream imagery to her current life issues. The following week she refused to participate in the artwork session where members drew pictures of a dream prior to sharing them. In the feedback after the pairs and artwork part of the session, this member (H) appeared to dominate the group and the following excerpt from the transcript illustrates other group members resisting her interpretations and recommending her not to feel responsible for everyone in the group:

H. *I feel awful about sharing my dream last week.*
Z. *You can't guarantee happy endings to dreams!*
A. *Has talking about the dream triggered difficult feelings?*
H. *I am concerned about how the group has received my dream...felt something horrible going wrong...feel everyone was disturbed by my dream...I want to reassure people that it wasn't a horrible dream...I feel that my dream which was a peaceful dream turned into a disturbing one unlike the outcome for Y's dream the week before...I feel I have been a negative damper on situation.*
D. *The effect of looking at dreams in a group can be quite disturbing...there is no agreement that we all go home happy.*
X. *The beginning of the session is the time to talk about how much is left from the previous week's work.*
Q. Challenges H. about how much she may have *'hurt us',* and suggests he (Q), *can handle any such hurt.*
F. Strongly says, *we are all responsible for our feelings and we can handle our feelings.*
H. *I feel wrongly guided about the dreamwork last week?*
G. *Do you really mean this?*
H. *I was made to feel uncomfortable last week and I feel I made others feel uncomfortable also.*
K. *You should check out if you think you have made people feel uncomfortable.*
F. *I think you should have sorted this out at the beginning of the session.*
H. *I think everyone else here knows everyone else except me.*

This interaction was probably the most difficult interpersonal sequence of the group and thereafter the group adopted a vigorous and reflective impatience with this group member. This was shown in the following interactions. She came to one or two more sessions and whilst she was able to speak freely, she was in turn challenged by other members if they felt she was unduly taking up 'group time' or if she was imputing thoughts and feelings to other members with which they disagreed. As previously described, the third group was markedly less conflictual, except, as noted, when gender became an explicit issue in relation to levels of self-disclosure within the group.

Group cohesion

Whilst group cohesion can be shown in many ways, such as regularity of attendance, the sharing of speaking roles and sensitivity to members' needs and aspirations, one aspect of cohesion that is noteworthy here was the regularity of remembrance of and reference to members' previous dream and fantasy imagery. On many occasions members spoke of previous dream and fantasy imagery and their interpretations. Members would refer to having incorporated an image from someone else's dream into their own. An example of this was X. referring to *'Y's cats* (from a dream not described in this book) *crept into my dream and one went into my bath and it was really dirty and they left all these bits in the bath...There were three cats.* I asked how she knew that they were X's cats and she said, *'they just were'.* Another spoke of 'stealing' someone else's dream image. Members reported, particularly in the later interviews, having dreams about the group and group members. However these tended not to be disclosed in the group. The above reported experience of shared visual imagery is evidence of a group cohesion and a group life. This sharing of imagery also represents the development of a common ownership of the imagery of at least some dreams. Such a collective identification supports my assertion of the group's development of a form of 'mini-archetype' or 'root metaphor' which the group incorporated as part of the narrative of both the individual and the group, and as such was part of the identity of the group both personally and collectively.

Leadership

The model of leadership used was that of facilitation. Facilitative leadership seeks to avoid the imposition of unnecessary structure upon the group and aims to allow members the maximum power possible within the group. The aim of this model is to 'make easy' the development of the group and the individual involvement of particular members. I planned and ran the group with a freelance groupwork colleague with whom I had worked with before in a groupwork setting which had incorporated some dreamwork. Whilst I came to the role with more interest in dreamwork per se, she had a greater interest in the group process than myself, as she was enrolled on a groupwork training course and was studying the process of the group for her assessment on that course. We usually took turns in introducing and finishing sessions and normally did not work on our own dreams in the group, although exceptions to that have already been noted. My colleague shared and worked on her dream material more openly than I did. We did however share current life information about ourselves and referred to any dreams we might have had in the opening 'rounds'. We shared fully the planning and debriefing before and after sessions and were in basic agreement about the aims and range of methods to be used by the groups. I have already focused on the main points of friction in the groups and how these included, among other issues, the role and dynamics of leadership. Whilst there was a basic harmony and trust between us as co-leaders there were small disagreements, for instance, about ending the sessions promptly, with my co-facilitator keen for a prompt finish both for the sake of having a clear structure and because of different domestic arrangements from myself. Our leadership was positively affirmed by most group members. One member referred to our:

bringing different perspectives which had been enhancing for the group ...felt leadership had been very valuable...had been valuable and gentle ...had developed a non-confrontational feel and had been supportive and guiding...I felt safe about sharing stuff.

Overall the facilitative style and the different groupwork experiences we brought to the group allowed the groups to develop effectively and provided an interesting dreamwork and groupwork experience for most of the participants. Probably the least successful operation of our role was in the second group where we allowed the group to deal with the difficult interpersonal situation. This strategy, however, is consistent with a facilitative mode of group leadership.

Self-disclosure

Smith (1980, p.19), a principal theorist and evaluator of the research literature on groupwork sees self-disclosure to the group and feedback by the group to the members as the central ingredients of encounter-type groupwork. Self-disclosure was a key issue in these dreamwork groups. The dream and its narration within a supportive group opens up a direct way into what a member described as the 'undefended self'. The dream image might not initially appear relevant to major preoccupations of the self but often in the narration itself or certainly in the ensuing discussion and action work, key possible insights, often accompanied by emotional pain and even traumatic memory, might be triggered. Different levels of self-disclosure by different members at different stages of the group were apparent. Already described was the 'peak' of self-disclosure towards the end of the third group when three female members shared intimate concerns from their personal life. Self-disclosure is obviously related to a number of factors, including the degree of trust in the leadership and in other group members, the level of security about confidentiality within the group and the member's previous experience of self-disclosure and its consequences for themselves within the group setting.

Anthropologists have found that trust, disclosure, dream content and cultural norms are related. For instance in the in the Sambian society of New Guinea, Herdt found three different discourses within which dream sharing took place. There was public talk, secret talk and private talk. Each of these discourses was structured in differing ways in relation to 'cultural rules, premises, expectations - frames that organise behaviour' (1987, pp.59-61). Public discourse was the most common, during which anyone in the social group could be present. Secret discourse referred to the communication of ritual secrets and was sexually segregated. Private discourse concerned personal secrets, typically about sexuality. Likewise, in the groups studied, members were often reticent about sharing both the dream content and particularly their understanding of a dream when it reflected their intimate or sexual relationships. Often a member would refer to the possible issue 'brought up' by the dreamwork in a form of personal code, indicating their understanding of the reference but not wishing to declare it more explicitly. For instance in the 'button' dream to be discussed in chapter seven, the dreamer refers to the button hanging by a thread as symbolising a much larger impending loss in her life. At that stage the group would only have been able to speculate as to what 'much greater impending loss' might refer to, though in this case the reference was made explicit by the member later in the group sequence.

Another time a dreamer referred to a member's suggestion as *'hitting the nail on the head'* but ventured then no further. Quite often a member would refer to a dream that they had had but wouldn't 'work on', for instance: *'I have had a dream but couldn't talk about it tonight'*. Likewise with the results of the guided fantasy sessions, members would not always share completely the experiences they had undergone in those fantasies. In terms of developing a climate conducive to self-disclosure I have already referred to the efficacy of dreamwork to encourage this given reasonable facilitation and a working group. Within these groups there were key times when self-disclosure developed, such as when members first discussed relationship issues, or when sexuality was discussed. However privacy was always retained and in the individual interviews I conducted following the end of the groups there were several references to dreams, often of a 'blue' nature that members had had about each other that had not been disclosed.

Evaluating the group

During the follow-up interviews I asked for members' evaluations of the group as a whole. The replies were generally very positive and partly reflect the fact that those members who only stayed for one or two sessions were not later available for interview. The following is a selection of evaluative comments. The first focuses on gender:

> *Particularly important was meeting new people and particularly the men in the group...felt able to be the same person with the men as with my women friends in the group...this is a new experience for me as my life has been very divided for me so far* (on gender lines).
> *Overall I do feel better about myself and part of this is the group...like a sea change...yes...and I give credit to the group for a lot of that.*
> *Particularly my reaction to conflict...it has underlined my avoidance of conflict and made me value confronting conflict...I felt I have become more honest about sharing how I feel.*
> *I feel the group has been invaluable in helping to show where I am or consolidating where I am ...I knew it would be the right thing to do to start working on my dreams in a group...it has been very interesting time for me...I have made a step that I have been on the verge of making for a long time and there will be other steps...all my dreams were indicative of that...either heralding it or giving me a handle on it in some way...the third group was twice as good as the second and the longer I was in the group I felt more comfortable...there was double the benefit in the third group* (this member was in the last two groups only)*...you have to make all that groundwork to get to the state of trust and security to get that benefit from what you disclose yourself...disclosing to a safe group of people is vital as it verbalises how you are feeling and you may not know how you are feeling...I have developed these intuitive connections due to the dream group.*
> *I will take dreaming much more seriously now...I won't dismiss it again...I want to dream...my subconscious has things to say to me...I don't feel frightened of dreams...now the fear is defused.*

This chapter has shown that the understanding of dream imagery does not occur within a social vacuum. Dream narration needs an audience and which parts of the dream and how the dream is narrated will depend upon the totality of the group climate. Trust, security and effective leadership are clear prerequisites for full disclosure of the remembered dream imagery in narration. As one dream narrator said above, *disclosing to a safe group of people is vital, as it verbalises how you are feeling and you may not know how you are feeling.* This quote well indicates the importance of the subjective feeling of safety in the facilitation of self-disclosure. The quote also shows that through narration the memory of the dream is enhanced and also that the narrative process itself promotes awareness of current feelings. In this way feelings are made manifest both to the narrator and to the group. The implicit feeling is made explicit through narrative and positive audience participation. Such trust and security are not however inevitable aspects of dreamwork practice in groups, as our experience in the second group shows.

Conclusion

This chapter has intended to show the importance of the group context and process in the understanding of the construction of meaning of the dream imagery reported by group members. I have tried to establish the crucial importance of facilitative leadership and the development of a safe and trusting environment. The importance of the group context to dreamwork reflects and confirms Tedlock's communicative theory, already identified, which stresses the importance of an analysis and awareness of the communicative context to our understanding of culturally based dreamwork practice. Such an awareness may often be implicitly or explicitly recognised by groupworkers. However I have aimed to show in detail how group processes, group events and personal meanings were interrelated and established.

7 Imagery, metaphor and language

Dreaming metaphors

This chapter develops further the idea of the dream image as being a form of metaphorical thinking. I also hope to show how the dream as metaphorical thought was understood in the groups by reference to the metaphorical basis of language, and to articulate the ritual and transformative process in this dreamwork. Once dream imagery is perceived as meaningful, as I have been proposing was generally the case in the studied groups, and particularly once the imagery of the dream had referential meaning ascribed to it, it becomes a *conscious* metaphor. Kracke has described the dream as being a, 'highly condensed, visual or sensory, metaphorical form of thinking' (1987, p.38). We have seen that he suggests that dream, like myth for Lévi-Strauss, is a kind of bricolage in that it gathers:

> from among the day residues ready to hand, and uses them to metaphorically express an emotional conflict, and to work out (or work towards) some resolution of it (1987, p.38).

The metaphorical nature of the dream prompts me to consider at this point the role of metaphorical thinking more generally. The dream is however not the only form of metaphorical thought. Lakoff and Johnson (1980) have analysed the metaphorical basis of our rationality and language. They have shown how our conceptual system is fundamentally metaphorical in nature and that metaphor implicitly structures our consciousness and action. Metaphor works by, 'understanding and experiencing one kind of thing in terms of another' (Lakoff and Johnson,1980, p.5). Moreover the metaphors that structure our consciousness are based on our everyday experience and are not arbitrary. For instance there is a relationship between our experience of spatial living, the 'spatial/orientational metaphors' such as 'up/down' and human states of wellbeing and sickness. States of happiness tend to be expressed as 'being up' in some form and likewise being dejected or sad is commonly metaphorically described as being 'down' in some way, as in the phrase 'I'm feeling down'. There is then a continuing dialogue and relationship between our physical and cultural experience and our understanding of the world through a metaphorically structured language-centred consciousness. We can then postulate that metaphorical thought is the basis of both dream imagery and conscious awareness. No wonder then that the two are linked! As Bourdieu says, '.. the mind is a metaphor of the world of objects which is itself but an endless circle of mutually reflecting metaphors' (1977, p.91). Further, we have seen how the insights generated by the group's reflection on the dream data are created and validated through the relating of this data to the metaphorical meanings contained in ordinary language usage.

I have already presented some instances of the meanings of dream imagery being generated through the creative and reflective use of pun, metaphor and idiom. The use of verbal puns in dream interpretation is a common form of interpretive device and can be traced as far back as Ancient Egypt. Mackenzie (1965, p.28) gives the example of the Ancient Egyptian word for buttocks being very similar to that of orphan. The Chester Beatty papyrus which is dated around 1350 B.C. and is the oldest written record of dream interpretation advises that dreaming of showing your buttocks is a sign of the death of one's parents. Another example of the use of puns as an interpretive device is that of the hearse and husband dream, presented in chapter five, in which the double meaning of 'pine' and 'pining' triggered a creative association. This dialogue between personal image and potential social meaning, as evidenced in the metaphors of ordinary language, such as in the above 'pine' and 'pining' metaphors, became a feature of group members 'making sense' of their dream imagery. Whilst such interpretive connections made by group members may seem imposed they appeared natural to members, as Charsley (1992, p.168) has also pointed out in his study of dream interpretation in contemporary African chuches.

The following example of a dream involving 'buttons' is also exemplary of this group and cultural process:

I am in a shop...I am either a customer or another shop assistant...I don't know which...another customer is asking for a special unusual button to go on a suit...a box of buttons is put on the counter and I see a lovely asymetrical black and white button which I have drawn and will describe to you in a minute...I draw her attention to it but she says she likes the buttons on my coat...laughter...I look down at them and think yes they are nice but they are not really unusual...the bottom one is coming loose and I pull the the thread to retighten it so I don't loose it...She goes on talking about her dress which is for a special occasion...I pick up a beautiful soft shiny dark women's hat in plaited straw which is notable for its quiet style and top quality...it really feels lovely...I am aware that it is not perhaps really the right colour to go with black which is what she said

102

the suit is and the colour she wants the button...she takes the hat from me and tries it on...I go on to look at shoes...I am conscious I would like the hat but the colour is quite wrong for me and I don't suit hats...I feel okay about passing it on to someone else...that's it...the button is oval...and the holes are set off to one side and it has green etched indentions in it in the centre...one is longer and the one on the sides are shorter and they are actually highlighted in white and so it is actually a black and white button...the white is just the detail of it.

The following edited transcript (edited due to length) will show the generation of meaning for the dreamer. P. is the dreamer:

P. It is an old-fashioned shop with the chairs people used to be able to sit on....good gracious...doesn't that go back...buttons are significant to me as my mother had a big box of buttons and when I was ill I was allowed to play with them...Oh Gosh...aye aye...I remember my mother had two boxes of buttons and when my mother died my father gave one to his brother's girlfriend at the time and I was furious...she had good sense and kindness and she gave me back the old buttons such as the mother of pearl and glass ones that belonged to my Grandmother...that is a memory that has come out of it.   Here the dreamer shares her remembrance with the group.
Q. Have you lost anything?
P. Not a material possession but I am in the process of losing something more fundamental but I don't want to talk about it.
F. How old are you in the dream?
P. There is a contradiction...I'm not sure if I am a customer or a shop assistant...I am still fascinated by design...I'm not sure in the dream as to my age...the hat is a bit shapeless ...but the quality of the straw is gorgeous...it is like silk...it is a wonderful colour ...between mushroom and bronze absolutely beautiful.
J. Were you recommending the hat?
P. Yes...she came in for a special button for her suit and we went through the buttons and I found a beautiful one which I thought would be lovely at the top of her suit but she wanted the one on my coat...but then if I had a coat on I must have been a customer...but that is being logical for a dream...she was getting something for a special occasion..hat...shoes...that is something I am quite capable of doing of spending time in a shop with a customer and becoming quite quite involved.
H. What is the other person like?
P. I have no sense of her except she is quite smartly dressed...she is quite a bit older than me...I feel she is not actually doing herself justice if she wants the button off my coat when there is this lovely one in the box.
Y. Does she remind you of anyone?

P. *Yes of my mother...at another level this could be me...I could be all the characters in the dream.*

Y. *Or the button?*

P. *Yes...I haven't worked on that...I had a sense she had to make up her own mind...I could only offer her areas of choice though I knew I wanted to have the hat...I would really love to wear that hat* (said emphatically).

Y. *How would you feel if you put it on?*

P. *Very self conscious...I feel everyone would look at it...I wouldn't want to draw such attention to myself...like I am doing now.*

T. *There's a sense of presence and liveness about you.*

P. describes colour of hat again...*bronze and shiny.* laughter.

Q. *It sounds valuable.*

P. *It has a quality of value about it...a silky quality...of straw...which seems to increase its value.*

G. *What makes you feel uncomfortable about wearing it?*

P. *How I would look in it...I have never been able to wear hats...I am the person you go to a shop with to cheer you up when she wears a hat...I have always had this kind of envy of people who can just put hats on and look wonderful.*

F. *Were you aware of this in the dream.?*

P. *Yes...other woman didn't value it...to put the hat on would make me the centre of attention...that is scarey and makes me feel being judged in some way...a judgement made of me...do I match up to a standard? am I able to wear a hat?*

Y. *Do you feel happy to wear a button?*

P. *Yes...absolutely must be something to do with things about fear...here something is coming to me* (sudden insight prompted by group suggestion) *there it is...about the intellectual and not feeling comfortable in very intellectual situations...I feel fascinated by them...would love to be there but feel utterly unable to be...that feels really powerful.*

I. *What brought that up?*

P. *Something about getting into the head...being above the head...*

Y. *Being ahead!...the hat is rather like you...rather beautiful and pink with a glow about it.*

P. *In car tonight...I thought am I the hat?...do I deny something in myself?*

Y. *What about mother?*

P. *Oh yes very strong connection about not putting yourself forward ...about keeping in the background...putting other people before yourself....being very kind...offering other people first.*

F. *You picked the button out for someone else...you tightened up your loose button.*

P. *It's about holding onto the things I already have and doing it in the easiest way because...just by pulling the thread.*

Q. It is quite strange...if the other person was your mother and she wanted the other buttons.

P. That would have been very typical of her...she would have worn the ordinary button...she liked buttons like that but she would have put them in a box.

Z. Like you.

P. I have just realised this (laughter).

T. Is the box a symbol for you?

P. The box I drew is...oh wait a minute...it is a very recurring symbol...I had another journey in a dream and I was looking for a box to put books in.

T. Do you put special things in boxes?

P. Yes...the button box was almost always kept for special times for cheering us up as children.

Y. Almost like you are going through now.

P. Yes...I need all the buttons I can find now.

F. But in a box rather than wearing them and putting yourself forward?

P. Yes well that is changing...as I would quite like to wear that button and that is what is quite scary...as I am acknowledging I don't have to go on being as I have been for so many years and I can actually be something else and I feel from inside me that that is okay and that is about wearing the button.

Q. And the hat?

P. And the hat (laughter)*...the button still feels safer to wear than the hat.*

F. You are beginning to be comfortable about wearing the button...you will need to see what will make you comfortable wearing the hat.

H. What is the predominant feeling in the dream.?

P. I am puzzled...I normally dream dreams that I can get immediate insight into...I woke up with the childish pleasure of going through this box...I feel quite young because of that.

W. It is also about being on display...as in the shop.

P. Yes...it is about display and providing a service and being there for others and not being the one that matters that is symbolised.

Z. The customer is always right?

F. (Identifying with being P.) *Not if they get your buttons they weren't right* (laughter)*...it is too easy for me to trade myself in and holding to what is right for me and not losing the boundary between being me and what I need to be in the outside world.*

T. I saw on your face that you might be the person or was who would have traded themselves in.

P. In the past I am the sort of person who would have chopped off the three buttons on my coat and given them away...but no way was I going to do that in the dream.

Z. Did you think of buying the button?

P. No isn't that sad!

D. You said this was sad?

105

P. I couldn't in a sense look after myself...buy myself something...treat myself.

I. We use metaphors...losing your buttons...buttoned up...bright as a button.

Q. The use of a button has a practical function.

P. They can be both practical and functional and decorative things...they don't have to be boring (P. speaks with real feeling as if a synthesis reached).

T. They control the opening and closing.

P. Provided the thread doesn't come off.

F. You sew them on so well.

P. That rings true and the rearranging is quite a palaver to remove them to somewhere else and is a long job and that is very symbolic as to what is happening at the moment.

I. To be the loose thread would be quite challenging.

P. The thread hanging on and loose could be cut and that would reduce the amount of thread holding the button and eventually it would come off...and (whispering)*I suspect it is already off or nearly?*

X. I feel the silky straw is very feminine.

P. I agree...it has the quality of femininity...I realised that the colour of the hat didn't suit me as it is too like my own colouring.

G. Therefore it wouldn't be so flamboyant.

F. Do you have any feelings about her not wanting the button/hat.

P. Not then...I have now...I have old feelings of not being appreciated...of having gone to all that trouble and not being appreciated...these are very very old feelings...there are very few feelings in the dream at all...I felt I was observing in the dream ...I was admiring the quality of that hat and that I would like it...I would covet it.

Q. Covet is a funny word.

P. I know it probably as I had to learn the ten commandments.

F. Thou shalt not covet your neighbour's hat! great laughter.

P. I feel that this is a very female-orientated dream...all the women getting ready and dressed for something.

F. Do you have a message for the women in dream.

P. You are not doing yourself justice...that's given me lots to think about.

The almost full transcript of the discussion of this dream shows the woman revealing major life preoccupations. The art deco button came to represent the dreamer's conflict between clothing and dress accessories as being for display or for utility. Latent feelings of having to always meet her own needs last and feelings of low self-esteem were expressed. She identified the loose button as representing a much greater impending personal loss in her life, that of her partner (stated in a later group session). As with other dreams the button symbol's potency was explored through the spontaneous consideration of the idiomatic usage of the 'button' and 'thread' symbols, such as in phrases as 'bright as a button', 'buttoned up', 'unbuttoned' and 'hanging by a thread'. At a cultural level the revealed interpersonal and sexual symbolism of buttons in this culture became a vehicle for developing personal understanding. Such a discussion of both learnt and experienced symbolism again gave the group the opportunity to critically reflect on questions of gender roles, socialisation and opportunities for empowerment by women. Through these examples from the dream narrations and discussions we can see how the dreamer and the group use significantly gendered and sexual symbols both unconsciously in dream material and consciously in group dialogue. The examples show that dream data consist of sets and sequences of images that are derived from everyday life and can reflect current concerns of the dreamer. The meanings generated are derived from this dialogue between self and group, and elicited by reflecting upon how we derive our dream imagery from our culture, and then in turn understanding our dream imagery by considering the use of metaphor in everyday language.

The promotion of ritual structure

So far I have described the meetings of dreamwork groups as events like those of any other discussion group or of people with certain interests in common. However, I show in the ethnography, the group dynamics, as structured, evoked a ritual process in which social change and personal development took place. Such a process of change is analysed by Turner (1974, pp.25-55) and I applied it in my M.Phil thesis (1986, and 1990, pp.45-57). In the dreamwork groups studied, although it was at the suggestion of the group leaders that the group should begin with the lighting of a candelabra and incense and finish with the blowing out of the candle, the suggestion was readily accepted by the group. The group event was framed by these acts. Within that time and space a typical set of procedures followed, which began with the 'opening round', which led into the discussion of one or more dreams in depth and often reached a climax with the 'acting out' of some part of the dream imagery through play, imaginative identification, meditation and artwork. As I show, within this process the transformation of the individual dreamer's symbolic image into a symbol for the group would frequently take place. The evidence for this is demonstrated in the ethnography in terms of the 'future life' of the symbol in the group's discourse and other members' dreams. In this way the group developed 'mini-archetypes' with which they developed the cultural identity of the group and generated significance for the dream and fantasy imagery. Within this created liminal (1) space separated from participants' other group involvements (Turner 1977, pp.37-9), the group spun its patterns of meaning through its absorption with, sensitisation to, and concentration on the narratively manifested images of the unconscious. The dream imagery became a form of theatrical event in which 'the meaning' was attempted to be read by the group as both audience and actors. The theatre analogy with dream is not new. Resnik (1987, p.1) uses it as his central metaphor to structure his analysis of the dream.

The ritual structure of the group event, bounded in time and space, is peopled by self-selecting seekers after their own meaning, who 'invent' and evoke symbols to contemplate, out of the resource of their own imag(e)inations. The image and its re-experiencing intersect and interpenetrate each other. The dream image is retrospectively recreated in new forms within the minds of the group members. The evoked meaning, reference and relevance for their lives of these manifest symbolic forms does not stay within the domain of the private world of the dreamer. Rather it is fashioned out of the group process of action and suggestion, and becomes the collective property of the group. The group then 'owns' the symbol having converted a private symbol into a public one. This transformation of understanding feeds into everyday life and the shape-shifting symbolic form feeds into the future dreams and discourses of the group's life. In a sense the original image of the unconscious becomes a symbol for the group through its cultural narration and appropriation by the group; thereafter it reclaims its metaphoric nature when referential meaning is ascribed to it. The everyday context of language and meaning has been transformed through a ritual process into a heightened and participative knowledge in which personal transformation has been sought and sometimes achieved.

The dreamwork examples described in this book, and particulary the last 'button' dream example, illustrate clearly the cultural re-working of dream imagery within and through the group process. Meaning is created, the self is invented in new, dazzling and disturbing garments. The groupwork processes allow and facilitate a play betwixt the ontological and the cultural. The self becomes temporarily the bidden image, and implicit, embodied emotion is evoked through the ritual performance of the groupwork task and setting. Consciousness becomes its imagery and opens up new fields of potential mental and affective connectedness.

Such new fields, encompassing both the narrator's mind and the consciousness of the group, is not however limitless. Meaning is not evoked from outside its context. Interpretive possibilities are those dormant within modern society's repertoire of potential meaning for material objects and cultural processes. An art deco button, presented within the dream in the this chapter, whilst capable in these groups of becoming a lived metaphor evoking and symbolising a gendered socialisation process, firmly remains a button within the terms understood normally for a button in society. Likewise a hearse is a car that carries dead people, even if in the fantasy world of the narrator/dreamer it represents a personal feeling state concerning the relationship with her partner. The interpretive processes recorded then are culturally contextualised and pertinent to our own modern or post-modern society, not to any society.

The personal and cultural symbol

In my discussion of the interrelation of metaphor and ritual I have described the ways in which dream symbols become living metaphors. As a study of individual and group enquiry into the meaning of dream imagery, this book is concerned with the meanings of both personal and cultural symbolism. There are many different theoretical views on the nature of such symbolism. Firth, for example, identified a symbol in a way reminiscent of the definition of metaphor already developed, as one thing representing or standing for another. He considered that the relationship between the symbol and that symbolised is that of the particular to the general and the concrete to the abstract. A lion then symbolises courage. In this view a symbol is a concrete indication of abstract ideas. Firth (1975, p.64) cites Langer who makes the following distinction: a sign signifies an object or a situation whilst a symbol makes us conceive of an idea. The relationship between a symbol and its referent is usually complex and as Jung has noted, there is often an inarticulate even unconscious aspect to our use of symbols:

> Thus a word or an image is symbolic when it implies something more than its obvious and immediate meaning. It has a wider unconscious aspect that is never precisely defined or fully explained. Nor can one hope to define or explain it. As the mind explores the symbol, it is led to ideas that lie beyond the grasp of reason. The wheel for instance may lead our thoughts towards the concept of a divine sun (1964, pp.20-21).

A symbol then refers to an abstraction that cannot be fully articulated. Firth also describes symbols as 'stores of meaning' (1975, p.81). Symbols can be potent agents of both personal and social change. Symbols, such as national flags and anthems, can be powerful instruments in the creation and maintenance of collective identity (Lewis 1977, p.6).

I have aimed to study the process whereby the personal symbols of the dreamer are transformed through group process into public symbols both for the group and for the individual. The group evocation of the meaning of the personal symbols, through gestalt and psychodrama for instance, transforms personal mental imagery into culturally contextualised sets of meanings. Dream imagery becomes 'good to think with' (Lévi-Strauss, quoted in Harris, 1986, p.13) or as Obeyesekere puts it:

> Personal symbols must be related to the life experience of the individual and the larger institutional context in which they are embedded (1981, p.13).

The cultural derivation of dream imagery in British society is shown, for example, in the frequent instance of group members using motifs and situations from television, such as the news or 'soaps', as fruitful day residue through which to re-enact symbolically their existential predicaments, in a transformed way. Moreover, I have shown how meaning is attributed to dream imagery through reference to culturally sanctioned collective understandings expressed in idiomatic language use. Thus the interplay between personal and cultural symbol lies at the heart of the data and its analysis. Whilst for Freud, as I outline in chapter two, the essence of dreamwork is the analysis of the transformations of deep motivation into the personal symbols of the dream, my study is that of the circular transformation of cultural symbol into personal symbol and then again into cultural symbol. As Obeyesekere says in countering the views of Leach (1958, pp.148-149), 'the symbol is both personal *and* cultural' (1990, p.22).

Notes

1 Liminal is a term taken from Van Gennep's (1960) study of rites of passage. In this study he proposed that a common structure of rites entailed a threefold process. First there was separation from the previous social state to a marginal or 'liminal' space, and finally the stage of return or re-aggregation back into a new position in the social structure. The liminal middle stage is the time and space in which personal and group change and reconstruction take place. I (Edgar, 1990, p.50) have elsewhere identified the use of liminal features within a western therapeutic community using Turner's (1977, pp.37-9) definition of the theory of liminality.

8 The social construction of the unconscious

Introduction

This chapter considers both the social action outcomes of dreamwork in the groups studied as well as developing further a social and political perspective on dreamwork.

Meaning and action

Throughout this book I have referred to, if not expanded upon, the effects of dreamwork on the lives of participants. This section intends to summarise the impact of dreamwork on members' lives and in so doing to present ethnographic evidence to show that, after Herdt, 'The productions of dreaming become absorbed and transformed into culture' (1987, p.82). This idea that dreams and social action intersect and develop each other has recently been developed by Jedrej and Shaw (1993, pp.8-9). They refer to Evan-Pritchard's classic study of Azande witchcraft in which Evans-Pritchard writes:

> The memory of dream images may influence subsequent behaviours and subsequent happenings may intrude upon the memory of dream images so that they conform to one another (1937, p.384).

This section also illustrates what Basso defines as the 'progressive function of dreaming' or the 'self becoming' (1987, p.101). The ethnographic evidence that I have derived from my study of the three dreamwork groups supports the proposition that dream and social action intersect with each other. My final evidence for this assertion will be presented under the following everyday categories: decision-making, self-esteem and 'coming to terms with life'. Whilst Evans-Pritchard (1937, p.381) presents interesting examples of the role of dreaming in providing

111

'acceptable accounts of action' (Jedrej and Shaw:1993, p.9) in the courtship behaviour amongst the Azande, no data was available in relation to sexual behaviours within the group.

Decision-making

Dreamwork clearly contributed to decision-making concerning both work and relationships of participants. The dreamwork helped clarify the issues through their public expression and exploration. The member who dreamt of her dead husband in the hearse in chapter five spoke, as already reported, of the dreamwork's contribution to her 'stock-taking' of the relationship. The imagery of the dream and work upon it in the group helped significantly towards making the relationship issues explicit to herself. This example is repeated in several of the reported pieces of dreamwork. The example of the dreamer who dreamt of a woman being forcibly and unhappily married, presented in chapter two, is one such example. The dreamer of the 'loaf' dream, to be presented later in this chapter, subsequently told the group that the dream had enabled her not to go to a job interview and had contributed to a significant rise in her self-confidence about her work ability. The person who dreamt of meeting her flatmate on the escalator, presented also in chapter five, resolved to express her negative feelings about their flat-sharing. A dreamer who dreamt of a beautiful bird (not presented in this book) shared in the interview how the experience of working on the dream had clarified for her the feelings she had about both her present job and her ambitions about developing alternative employment.

Self-esteem

The categories which I am using obviously overlap in so far as, for example, self-esteem is an inseparable aspect of decision-making. The 'button' dream, presented in the last chapter, provides a good example of how the dreamer reflected on the gendered effect of her parenting and socialisation upon her life to date. Moreover there were indications through the transcript that she was changing through the process as:

> *Well that is changing...as I would quite like to wear that button and that is what is quite scarey...as I am acknowledging I don't have to go on being as I have been for so many years and I can actually be something else and I feel from inside me that that is okay and that is about wearing the button.*

The effect of this piece of dreamwork on the dreamer is later summarised by her in the interview:

The meaning was getting in back in touch with my childhood self...the carefree-ness of it...the pleasure that buttons could bring...also something I shared with my mother brings me close to her...brings me right within myself and takes me back to when I was in bed and sick and I had the button box and I would sort them out and make patterns and that was how I got through childhood illnesses and it reminds me that I had inner resources and at the time of the dream it was very important to remind myself of that as I was about to start on my own again...the box is within and is Pandora's box!

The dreamer defines the meaning of the dreamwork in terms of her rediscovery of her own inner resources. These inner resources are affirmed through remembrance of her childhood and her development of coping capacities at that time. Another example of 'self-esteem' being the focus of the dreamwork is the 'mother's teeth' dream presented in chapter five. During this piece of dreamwork the dreamer explores the possibility of the teeth representing her 'social front' and, following on from that identification, her angry and vulnerable feelings emerge. By the end of the dreamwork she has made an affirmation of herself and of her own worth. An example from my own dreamwork in the group is when I shared a dream snippet in the second group in the beginning round. In this I dreamt that my car had a six inch dent on the driver's side of the car. My interpretation of the image was that it was related to the group session the week before when my leadership style and purpose had been confronted as described in chapter six. That process had somewhat unnerved me and the dream image seemed to reflect the extent of the damage to my reputation as a facilitator in the group and to my personal self-esteem. I related this in the group session as the dent in the car not being too serious in terms of the function of the car and talked about how one might expect 'bumps and knocks' in life.

'Coming to terms with life'

If, as the revised psychoanalytic perspective suggests, dreams are a 'manifest problem-solving and integrative process that takes place as metaphorical thought', then we could expect that a study of the dreamwork in the groups would reveal an abundance of members 'coming to terms with life', such as was also discussed in chapter four when I reviewed studies of dreaming relevant to the caring professions. Most of the dreams and their accompanying dreamwork already presented can be seen to fit this 'coming to terms with life' category. Whether their problem is one of relationships or one of work and career issues, dreams and dreamwork as described and analysed can be crucial in the identification by the dreamer, of an explicit awareness of the situation, and can often be formative in developing a resolution to change themselves or their situation. Whilst all the examples of dreams so far explored have been of single dreams, members did occasionally experience a dream sequence, and then interpreted the sequence and the transformations of imagery within the sequence. One member had several dreams involving animals including one with lots of sleek black cats that clung sinuously to her body and which she was unable to get rid of. Another dream involved a bear, cats and birds:

> *There was a bear in a toilet with another woman who is on the right. ...a big bear comes...she runs one way and me another and she finds the way out...I am in this little alcove area behind the door...the shambling bear coming through the door...ugh...to get me...there is no door on the alcove...another door is round the corner and I get it to protect me and partly shield me from the bear and then some people come to rescue me and I come out and they are planning to have a meal at a cafe...then I am with some family...there are some houses including mine and there is a big old building...a similar situation to near mine...in the dream it is different to mine and there are all these black cats...a great herd of them and they have multiplied and live in this building and we shoo them away without any trouble...they run away...across the fields there are these lights coming to rescue me from the cats...these points of lights streaming across fhe ields and in the vanguard of the lights are these lovely little birds...green yellow and a bit of red...then I woke up.*

In this instance the dreamer felt that the progression from the previous cat dream and the bear image in the above dream to the image of lights and birds coming towards her represented a movement in herself to a more optimistic stance towards her life. The dreamer had recently experienced a distressing divorce and felt some of the feelings engendered by those events were represented for her in the dream imagery and their transformation. These findings offer clear evidence as to when, how and what effect dreams have on the lives of dreamers. In this sense this book shows the intersection of dream and reality in Western society in a way foreshadowed by Evans-Pritchard.

A social and political perspective

As I wrote in the introduction, the dreamwork movement in Western industrialised societies began in the United States in the 1970s as an offshoot of the personal growth movement. The essence of this movement is that the dream image is an important aspect of the self and is significant in developing an understanding both of oneself and of one's world. Writers such as Garfield (1974) popularised ways of working in groups with dreams. For this she drew substantially on anthropological research into how non-literate peoples viewed dreaming, often in an altogether more positive way than in the West.

Social dreaming

Ullman (1979, pp.92-116) and subsequent other writers have written about how to run dreamwork groups. In the last few years, dreamwork groups have mushroomed in the UK and can now be found in most large cities. The women's movement especially has explored the dream and the products of active imagination (Ernst and Goodison, 1981, p.161; Butler and Wintram, 1991, pp.52-54) with a view both to a deeper understanding of female personal and social identity, and also as a way of challenging negative patterns of gendered socialisation. In particular the writing and guided imagery exercises of Ernst and Goodison have inspired and taught groups of women, including survivors of different forms of sex abuse. Shohet (1985, pp.83-120) has reported the creative and significant use of dreamwork groups in schools and communities. He also writes about the use of dreams for specific consciousness raising purposes such as overcoming racial prejudice.

Lawrence (1989) started 'social dreaming' meetings in which the aim was to explore social issues through dreaming and dream discussion. This work was inspired by Charlotte Beradt's book 'The Third Reich of Dreaming' (1968), in which Beradt studied how the dreams of people in Nazi Germany reflected the development of totalitarianism on the human psyche, and how the effect of this totalitarianism became subsequently manifest in people's behaviour and psychological patterns. Lawrence, referring to Bettleheim's essay in the Beradt volume, writes, 'They (dreams) evince what people really believe the political system is like and so have a prophetic quality' (1989, p.76). Lawrence was also influenced by anthropological evidence as to how, for instance, Taiwanese aboriginal hunters were strongly influenced as a group by dreams. The social dream meetings started by Lawrence and conducted in several countries, were intended for a wide range of professional groups. The main result, at least in the UK, seem to have been a focus, expressed through dream imagery initially, on Government cutbacks and redundancy. Collective anger at these developments was evoked through the process. Members reported becoming able to reflect in a deeper way on their professional work and roles. At the end of the project Lawrence wrote:

It (can) be hypothesised with more firmness that it is possible to have dreams which speak of our unconscious fears and anxieties about the society in which we live. The individual dreams around certain basic themes such as the family, work and relationship with parents, and significant others. Society however only exists 'in the mind' as a construction of individuals based on their experiences of relationships with others with whom they happen to be connected (1991, p.268).

Lawrence sees 'social dreaming' as a process in which, significantly, the meaning of a dream is not established until the **social** (my emphasis) meaning is established. Such a view, coming out of experimental work at the Tavistock clinic, is a very important development which undermines the C20 psychological paradigm of dreaming only being of relevance, if of any relevance at all, to the individual. Moreover dreaming has recently been seen as a way, not just of understanding the self as some kind of isolated ego, but as a way of becoming aware of how social structure and social stereotyping have been constituent factors in self development (Ullman, 1989, pp. 281-282). Fromm has described this area of our group lives as the 'social unconscious' (1955, quoted in Ullman, 1989, p.281). A sociological or anthropological perspective on dreaming (Ullman, 1989) can therefore unmask prevailing personal and group myths and stereotypes about men and women and black and white people for example. I suggest (Edgar, 1992, p.57) therefore that dreamwork can be used in consciousness raising or empowerment group work initiatives as well as in the perhaps more typical 'therapeutic' or personal growth type groupwork settings.

A social and political perspective in the groups

The interpretive purpose displayed in the dreamwork groups was influenced by social theory as well as by psychological theory. A feminist perspective was the most manifest political and social perspective in the interpretive process, and has already been articulated, as in chapter five in the 'binary analysis' discussion of the 'crumbling tooth' dream in which the dream evokes for the dreamer the memories of a sexually harassing encounter. A feminist perspective, in relation to dreamwork, is concerned, through its focus on personal imagery, with an analysis of the oppression of women in a patriachical society as well as with the practical empowerment of women within their actual lives. Such a perspective approaches any interpretive position in relation to dream imagery as possibly needing to be critiqued from a feminist standpoint. Moreover such socially constructed systems of meaning as interpretive frameworks for dreamwork are continually being re-evaluated as shown by the dream interpretation example presented in chapter four in the family therapy section. Likewise the feminist interpretations evident in the examples from my dream data, such as in the following data, similarly illustrate the point:

> *It started with me driving the car...my boyfriend was there...we arrived in a country village...my little boy went off to the shops...I bought a loaf of bread* (Y. comments later she is always organising people buying bread for her family) *I went into bookshop for a job interview which I was not very interested in but I had heard about...I went through to the back garden...went through back garden...I love bookshops but I am scared of them...I used to have the shits in the library...still sometimes do...but I love books...it was very warm in the shop...there was an attractive woman sitting at table...she was a secretary...I came up to her*

...I said 'I believe there is a job'...she said...if you just wait there... the owner is coming back soon'...it was lunchtime...couples come in dancing and kissing...my boyfriend and his ex-wife...having a frictional conversational ...they are very unhappy...they are attacking each other...I stood there just observing with this large loaf of bread...getting stickier...the icing all dripping down onto my smart suit....waiting ages...went up to secretary...again I said 'I don't really want to do this job anyway'.

This dream reflects the woman's concern with her current job situation and an impending interview. The unpacking of meanings from this dream imagery was long and complex and involved the member reflecting on her present job situation and feelings about current and past key relationships. Overall she felt the dream reflected her anxiety and fear of assessment linked to a present fragility of self image in the domestic sphere. By doing a gestalt identification with the icing on the bread she got in contact with very basic feelings and perceptions about her mother and her mother's expectations of her. Throughout the discussion and exercise a powerful theme for the group was the spontaneous discovery of the various metaphors of bread embedded in ordinary language use such as 'using your loaf', being 'kneaded', being 'proved', 'being good enough to eat', a 'bun in the oven', and 'loafing about'. These became both humorous asides but also powerful metaphorical summaries, via the puns on, for example, 'being needed' and 'being proved', of the dreamer's self state and current self image. She, during this session, developed an identification with the bread symbol which became a multi-vocal symbol of the self capable of many different amplifications of meaning. The 'bread' metaphor became then, through enactment, a lived metaphor for the group and was often referred to in group discussions as exemplifying the profound and transformative effect of working with dream symbols in the group context.

Whilst the group in this session was focused on assisting the dream narrator and playing with these 'bread' metaphors, the issues arising from the discussion are reflective of structural, in this case patriarchical, aspects of culture. The dreamer identified the linking of the bread and the icing and the interview with her concern about maintaining her physical attractiveness and avoiding her male partner's rejection if she became overweight. The group on this occasion focused on affirming the innate attractiveness of the dreamer, without reference to male expectation, and the ability of the dreamer to define herself - to become 'her own loaf'! Any structuralist perspective that is concerned with explaining and correcting social inequality, whether it be that of class, gender, race, ability or sexuality, has to consider the role of stereotyping of the oppressed 'other'. Whilst individuals may well be conscious of their ability to negatively stereotype women, black or gay people, the way the dream image is explained and identified may well be viewed as discriminatory. With regard to the example of racial stereotyping, Jung's analysis of the 'black man' as representing the 'shadow', or inferior, personality is now rightly seen as racist by contemporary commentators on Jung's work. Wehr, for instance, makes this point as well as highlighting the inappropriatenss of this part of Jungian theory in the analysis of a black person (1988, p.63). The potential for white people to, perhaps inadvertently, interpret dream imagery in a racist way was possibly also illustrated in the group. A white women dreamt:

I was standing in a people-carrier...a train or a metro...that was jam packed with people...I was standing by a sliding door and down the platform came a very handsome and tall negro and he had both legs down one side of his trouser...the right trouser leg was hanging...both legs were down the left side...he was shuffling along and not making very good progress...the right trouser was hanging loose...flopping at the side...we made space for him in the people carrier...I was friendly with all the people on the people carrier...everyone was very amused about this character we knew he was an alien...he didn't know how to handle human clothes...we all laughed.

Clearly the dream is portraying a negative image of a black person in the dream. The black man is 'alien', socially extremely inept having two legs down one trouser leg. He is also very handsome. Here is the image in a white woman's dream of a socially inferior, but very handsome black man. Perhaps it is not surprising that in both the discussion about the dream and in the individual interview, the image of this black man is interpreted as being related to her 'physical', sexual nature, to the 'dangerous and unscrupulous part of her masculine side'. The black man then is interpreted as standing in this typically negative, or partly negative, role for the white woman. He embodies the repressed and 'darkly' dangerous sexual nature of the white women. If such a dream image was present in the dream of a black person, male or female, what difference would and should that make? In the above dream it is possible to hypothesise that the dreamer is using historically constructed and racist stereotypes, certainly to interpret (with others) the image and even more problematically to 'create' the image.

Whilst an interpretation is definitely the responsibility of the dreamer and of the group, it is a much more problematic question to consider if the dreamer is 'responsible' for the dream image itself. Can the dream be said then to express intentionality? This is not a new problem. Gell (1992, p.57) refers to an incident concerning a missionary in the 1920s in Brazil in which an Indian demands compensation for his lost pumpkins, solely, as it transpires, on the evidence that the Indian had dreamt that the missionary had stolen his pumpkins! To the Indian the dream expressed clearly the desire of the missionary to 'steal' his pumpkins. A further and perhaps more bizarre example refers to a reported case in the USA where a man was accused of a murder in Chicago on 12th October, 1980 solely on the basis of his dream report. The police in this case considered that his dream account contained information that he could only have gained had he actually committed the murder (Bershady and Wagner-Pacifici, 1989, p.8)! At the time of the writing of the paper the authors reported that at the first trial the Jury 'believed the so-called dream was a deflected confession' (1989, p.11). However, this judgement was overruled by the Appeal Court, which was in turn overruled by the Illinois Supreme Court, which ordered a re-trial. Within the various twentieth century psychological systems I have introduced in this chapter there would be a consensus that the ego is not responsible for an action in the dream, since the dream image, while it might represent overt or covert wishes, does not represent 'reality' and 'real' morally responsible behaviour. Freud asked himself the same question:

> ..is the ethical significance of suppressed wishes to make light of wishes which, just as they lead to dreams, may some day lead to other things... I have not considered this side of the problem further. I think, however, that the Roman Emperor was in the wrong when he had one of his subjects executed because he had dreamt of murdering the Emperor. He should have begun by trying to find out what the dream meant...I think it is best, therefore, to acquit dreams (1955, p.658).

So whilst the ego is not held in Westernised society to be responsible for the dramas, perversions and cruelties that the dreaming subject experiences, the person is responsible for any interpretation accepted of the dream image. These interpretive frameworks are historically and culturally constructed and may contain negative stereotyping of oppressed groups. The political and cultural analysis of the whole process of dream interpretation is still perhaps in its infancy.

Implications for groupworkers

How meaning is defined and owned in dreamwork groups or groups that occasionally consider member dreams is extremely significant and raises core issues of personal and social power in groups. The aim of dreamwork groups, as I have led and experienced them is to facilitate members' reaching their own satisfactory understanding of a dream image or sequence, but with help and occasional challenge from the group. The group and its individual members, should not attempt to impose an interpretation, as happened occasionally in our group around the issue of sexual interpretation. Such a rule is equally significant for mixed race groups and in groups where different forms of sexual orientation are expressed. Clearly racist and homophobic attitudes are not acceptable and would be inimical to the development of the trust that is needed in such groupwork. However, conscious discrimination is easier to manage and confront than the expression of less conscious and negative stereotyping of black people, women and gay people by group members. Such stereotypical imagery and thought is embedded in our consciousness through our socialisation. Groupworkers using this approach need to be sensitive to the appearance of problematic stereotyping within dream imagery and/or members' stereotypical projection onto other members' imagery. The cardinal rules seem to be to facilitate the dreamer staying in control of the direction of the group discussion, and for the group to recognise that, paradoxically perhaps in relation to Perl's theory of dreaming, 'we' are not 'responsible' for our dream creations in the same way as we are for our conscious thoughts.

9 Conclusion

Anthropological findings

I have intended to show how both dream image and narrative discourse are fundamentally metaphorical in nature. Such a metaphorical kinship explains how the dream interpretation process was often most successful when there was a 'playing' by the group with the metaphorical possibilities of the dream image as embedded within idiomatic language use. The findings of the ethnography have shown how the dreamtime of the groups is in a sense a liminal space outside of ordinary time. The sense of time in the groups, through their focusing on the interaction of dream and reality, is condensed, stopped, reversed and apparently overcome. The dream is a story that you tell yourself without knowing why; a story told with shyness or openness that becomes more alive once it is served back by the group and the facilitators. The dream becomes more of a reality through its public shaping in front of an audience. The group, as co-workers and audience then, are vital to the emergence of meaning, and this helps situate dreamwork firmly as a social activity. A ritualised reality is created within the liminal space of the dreamwork groups. The normal sense of self is transformed. The 'I' can become a bird, a button, a hearse for example. How does this take place? I have shown that the dream imagery is a metaphorical potential for the dreamer and that, as these images are narrated, they are increasingly subject to social and cultural manipulation. The dream is given body through the process of imag(e)ing. The first telling is usually incoherent and then develops a progressive coherence and clarity through its shaping within the group. Obeyesekere suggests that we utilise cultural forms to weave the dream imagery into a narrative plot, which he calls 'emplotment':

> This term (emplotment) enables us to designate the process whereby the dream thoughts are creatively organised into a narrative that can, in some instances at least, stand on its own as a story. To miss this is not simply to miss something significant about dreams; it is to miss understanding

an aspect of cultural creativity that can transform deep motivation into narrative (1990, p.267).

The construction of a communicable and ordered narrative out of the bizarrely ordered fragments of often ill-remembered dreams confronts participants and a researcher with the fundamental experience of narrative creativity. The experience of first defining the dream image to oneself and then translating the imagery in all its multifarious and potential definitions into a communicable linguistic entity goes beyond baffling and taxing the imaginative resources of the dreamer. It transforms the most subjective of experiences into an object for viewing and absorbing by the group as well as by the original dreamer. This process of objectivisation, of the self becoming an object within and for the world, as defined by Csordas (1990, p.40), reaches its zenith in these dreamwork groups.

The dream imagery, on occasions, is transformed into artistic statement and performed dramas. Such an objectivisation of the self was noted by group members as the following quote shows. In a dialogue reported in detail in chapter six, one of the members describes the dream as, *'a story or picture and therefore the dream is out there and can be worked on quite safely'*. The process of telling stimulates the memory. Yet an evolved and more coherent narrative is a combination of dream fact and real fiction as the narrator attempts to fuse their dreamworld and reality. Within the ritualised reality of the dreamwork groups, metaphor and meaning is made in front of members' eyes. The ritual process of the group and its methods evoke both distant and near realities. Above all the ritual setting evokes feelings, often buried, inchoate and half recognised as in the hearse/pining dream.

This book, as well as looking at the private production of imagery considers the emotions shared and the feelings generated as the enlivened and fading images are chased and hunted by the group. The symbols evoked and fashioned within the group join feelings to thoughts. Turner (1974, pp.55-6) showed in his analysis of ritual process how social values are collectively owned through their fusion with everyday physical phenomena. The evoked symbols and root metaphors of the narrator and the group generate novel meaning through the creativity and multi-vocality of the symbol within the ritually constituted time and place. The work of the ritual is achieved in generating the connectedness of dream imagery to everyday reality. This connectedness is made possible through the self-enhancing power of the symbol. We can observe a transformative process as the button of the dream, for example, becomes a multi-faceted icon for the gendered life story of the individual. The button as a metaphor is created before our eyes; meaning darts in and through suggestion and verbal play. Reality itself becomes a meaningful metaphor. The dreamer/narrator sees various vignettes of her life history as in a cinema. This evocative retrieval process cannot be done alone but only within the group context and through the production of a liminal space in which communitas, being the

122

egalitarianism typical of liminality, means an equality before the imaginative productions of the unconscious.

An understanding of the dreamwork group as a ritual process is then a key perspective in the elucidation of the transformative process which can occur in such a dreamwork group. By the end of the twenty-nine group sessions the original members had become expert imagemakers, personally and collectively metamorphosed through the use of metaphors. They had become facilitators of their own personal transformation through their growing expertise in working with dreams. They had learnt to tell the stories of the self and to articulate a personal ontology. In this sense they had learnt to realise the self. Such an empowerment of the self was achieved through a developing mastery of the personal and social meaning of their own metaphors as developed in and through the group process.

Overall this book contends that the culturally constructed meaning of the dreams in the groups did not lie within the original identity of the dreamt symbols. Rather the meaning was evoked, as I have shown, through the group process. In this sense the dream is not solely a text waiting for a textual analysis. Rather it is a created and lived performance. Viewing the dream and its narration solely as a text may tell us much, but it will not tell us all. The meaning of the button or the bulb images, lay in their cultural contextualisation by the dreamer and the group. In themselves they then meant nothing! Symbols then can be said to mean nothing other than what is produced by the audience and the group interaction.

If this perspective is correct, then dreams do not represent the fundamental truths of the personality as psychoanalysis asserts. Rather they are formed through the bricolage process and their essential nonsense is made culturally meaningful solely through the group process. Such a perspective positions social anthropology, and perhaps sociology, in a powerful position to claim an increased role concerning the elucidation of the processes and outcomes of dream interpretation in modern society. Whilst anthropology has in the past only considered the dreams of bounded groups in the third world as of cultural significance, this work asserts the significance of dream and its elucidation in modern society as a vital source of understanding and information about the culturally constituted and becoming self.

The caring professional

This book has also aimed to show caring professionals that dreams and dreamwork are a fruitful resource for practice. I have not written a step by step manual on dreamwork as many such examples exist and have been referred to. Rather I have aimed to demonstrate, through a detailed example, the creative process and potential of a dreamwork practice that has drawn on a variety of techniques, such as gestalt and imagework. Such techniques at a basic level are not difficult to learn to use and many counsellors and groupworkers will be familiar with some or all of them. Moreover, there are longer training programmes available for advanced work in areas such as gestalt and psychodrama.

I have wanted to demonstrate that dream imagery, whether derived from a deliberate focusing on dreams by a worker or as the result of a spontaneous disclosure by a service user, can be a valuable resource for workers in the caring professions. Service users, patients, residents and clients of the caring professions will sometimes speak of a dream they have had, usually as an aside during an interview, conversation or group session with a professional. I hope this book will sensitise workers to possible ways of understanding such dream imagery and also encourage them to begin the practice of working with dreams.

Practice has been conceptualised as work within several different contexts, such as in counselling, groupwork, family therapy, supervision and team-building. I have considered diverse fields of service users such as the terminally ill, refugees, siblings of children with severe learning difficulties and people transiting through such life changes as becoming a parent. Research and practice findings described throughout this book have shown that dream imagery reflects both the individuals' metaphorical picturing of their situation and how these sets of imagery can be identified as potential patterns that can be used to define personal change, such as in the study on expectant fathers.

Overall the task of the dreamworker is to facilitate through the group process, the dream narrator's ability to identify relevant themes from their personal, often bizarre, imagery. Such an understanding arrived at from the group's contemplation of the narrated dream images is the aim, not always of course achieved, nor disclosed by the narrator to the group.

In this book I have presented dream imagery and dream interpretation as a social and political activity that has the potential to reflect political structures as shown in my reference to Beradt's and Lawrence's work in the last chapter. Dream interpretation is also a contested site for the contemporary generation of meaning, as in my portrayal of a feminist perspective within the groups I studied. In this sense I would argue against an absolute set of meanings being defined within a culture with which to understand dream imagery. Rather, dreamwork is a culturally-specific process that changes over time and is a social, political, personal and professional resource of intriguing, and usually neglected potential.

Appendix

This appendix presents in tablular form some basic data about the members of the dreamwork groups. Data is shown for members who stayed for more than three group meetings. An asterix* indicates an estimation. In the first column 'attendance': 1,2,3 relate to the first, second and third groups. Age is represented as at time of interview, July 1990. Occupational identity is defined partly by the member and partly by my categorisation, e.g. admin.

Table 2: Membership details

	Attendance	Gender	Age	Occupation	Relationship status	Children
A.	1. 2. 3.	F.	45	Counsellor	Cohabitation	Yes
B.	1.	F.	25*	Student	Single	No.
C.	1. 2. 3.	F.	44	Counsellor	Single	Yes
D.	1. 2. 3.	M.	60	Retailer	Single/ divorced	Yes
E.	1. 2. 3.	F.	54	Counsellor	Single/ divorced	Yes
F.	2. 3.	F.	46	Admin.	Single/ divorced	Yes
G.	2. 3.	F.	45	Admin.	Married	Yes
H.	2.	F.	54	Retired/ Nurse	Single	Yes
I.	2.	M.	50*	Retired	Single/ divorced	Yes
J.	2. 3.	M.	45	Engineer	Married	Yes
K.	2. 3.	F.	26	Unemployed	Single	No

Bibliography

Abraham, K. (1979), 'Dreams and Myths: a Study in Folk Psychology' *Clinical Papers and Essays on Psychoanalysis,* Hogarth Press, London.

Assagioli, R.(1967), *Jung and Psychosynthesis,* Psychosynthesis Research Foundation, New York.

Assagioli, R.(1980),*Psychosynthesis,* Wildwood House, London.

Bahaullah .(1945), *The Seven Valleys and the Four Valleys,* Ali-Kuli Khan (trans) Bahai Publishing Trust, Illinois.

Barrett, D. (1991), 'Through a glass darkly', *Omega,* vol. 24, part 2.

Bastide, R. (1966), 'Sociology of the Dream' in Grunebaum V. and Caillois R. (eds.), *The Dream and Human Societies,* University of California Press, Berkeley.

Basso, E. (1987), 'The Implications of a Progressive Theory of Dreaming' in Tedlock, Barbara (ed.), *Dreaming: Anthropological and Psychological Interpretations,* Cambridge, University Press,Cambridge.

Benson, J. (1987), *Working More Creatively with Groups,* Tavistock, London.

Beradt, C. (1968), *The Third Reich of Dreams,* Quadrangle Books, Chicago.

Berne, E. (1964), *Games People Play,* Grove Press, New York.

Bershady, H. and Wagner-Pacifici, R. (1989), *'Portents or Confessions: Authoritative Readings of a Dream Text',* The American Sociological Association Conference, San Francisco, California,

Bettelheim, B. (1974), *A Home with a Heart,* Thames and Hudson, London.

Bible, The New English (1961), First Edition, Oxford University Press, Oxford.

Bourdieu, P. (1977), *Outline of a Theory of Practice,* Cambridge University Press, Cambridge.

Brown, A. (1979), *Groupwork,* Heineman, London.

Buckholz, M. (1990), 'Using dreams in family therapy', *Journal of Family Therapy,* vol. 12, no. 4.

Butler, S. and Wintram, C. (1991), *Feminist Groupwork*, Sage, London.

Caplan, P. (1988), 'Engendering knowledge: the politics of ethnography (Part 2), *Anthropology Today*, vol. 4, no. 6.

Carrithers, M. (1982), 'Hell-fire and urinal stones: an essay on Buddhist purity and authority,' in Krishna G. (ed.), *Contributions to South Asian Studies 2*, Oxford University Press, Delhi.

Castaneda, C. (1970), *The Teachings of Don Juan*, Penguin, London.

Catalano, S. (1987), *'Developmental Differences in the Dream Content of Normal and Emotionally Disturbed Adolescents'*, Unpublished D.S.W. dissertation, Boston College Graduate School of Social Work.

Cernovsky, Z. (1988), 'Refugees' repetitive nightmares', *Journal of Clinical Psychology*, vol. 44, no. 5, September.

Cernovsky, Z. (1990a), 'Escape stress, sleep disorders, and assimilation of refugees', *Social Behaviour and Personality*, vol. 18, no. 2.

Cernovsky, Z. (1990b) 'Group nightmares about escape from ex-homeland', *Journal of Clinical Psychology*, vol. 46, no. 5. September.

Charsley, S. (1992), *Wedding Cakes and Cultural History*, Routledge, London.

Charsley, S. (1992), 'Dreams in African Churches' in Jedrej, M. and Shaw, Rosalind (eds.), *Dreaming, Religion and Society in Africa*, Brill, Leiden.

Cividini-Stranic, E. (1986), 'The group dream in group psychotherapy', *Group Analysis*, vol. 19.

Cook, C., Caplan, R. and Wolowitz, H. (1990), 'Non-waking responses to waking stressors: dream and nightmares', *Journal of Applied Social Psychology*, vol. 20, no. 3.

Corbin, H. (1966), 'The Visionary Dream in Islamic Spirituality', In Von Grunebaum G. and Callois R.(eds.),*The Dream in Human Societies*, University of California Press, Berkeley

Crapanzano,V. (1975), 'Saints, Jnun, and dreams: an essay in Moroccan ethnopsychiatry', *Psychiatry*, 38.

Csordas, T. (1990), 'Embodiment as a paradigm for anthropology', *Ethos*, vol. 8.

Cushway, D. and Sewell, R. (1992), *Counselling with Dreams and Nightmares*, Sage, London.

D'Andrade, R. (1961), 'Anthropological Studies of Dreams', in Hsu. F. (ed.), *Psychological Anthropology: Approaches to Culture and Personality*, Dorsey, Homewood, Ill.

Darou, W. (1990), 'The use of dream work in supervision', *The Clinical Supervisor*, vol. 8, no. 2.

Devereux, G. (1966), 'Pathogenic dreams in Non-Western societies', in Grunebaum, V. and Caillois R. (eds.), *The Dream and Human Societies*, University of California Press, Berkeley.

Devereux, G. (1969), *Reality and Dream. Psychotherapy of a Plains Indian*, New York, International Universities Press.

Devereux, G. (1980), *Basic Problems of Ethnopsychiatry*, University of Chicago Press, Chicago.

Domhoff, G. (1985), *Mystique of Dreams: A Search for Utopia through Senoi Dream Theory,* University of California Press, Berkeley.

Douglas, M. (1975), *Implicit Meanings: Essays in Anthropology,* Routledge and Kegan Paul, London.

Douglas, T. (1976), *Groupwork Practice,* Tavistock, London.

Duerr, H. (1985), *Dreamtime: Concerning the Boundary between Wilderness and Civilisation,* Blackwell, Oxford.

Edgar, I. (1986), '*An anthropological analysis of Peper Harow therapeutic community with particular reference to the use of myth, ritual and symbol',* M.Phil. thesis, University of Durham.

Edgar, I. (1989), *'Dreaming as Ethnography',* the Association of Social Anthropologists Annual Conference:Anthropology and Autobiography, York, England.

Edgar, I. (1990), 'The Social Process of Adolescence in a Therapeutic Community', in Spencer P. (ed.), *Anthropology and the Riddle of the Sphinx: Paradoxes of Change in the Life Course,* ASA Monographs 23, Routledge, London.

Edgar, I. (1992), 'The dream in groupwork practice', *Groupwork,* vol. 5, no. 2.

Edgar, I. (1994), 'Dream Imagery becomes Social Experience: The cultural elucidation of dream interpretation', in Deluz, Ariane and Heald, Suzette (eds.), *Anthropology and Psychoanalysis: An Encounter Through Culture,* Routledge, London. .

Eggan, D. (1952), 'The manifest content of dreams: A challenge to social sciences', In *American Anthropologist* vol.54.

Eichenbaum, 1. & Orbach, S. (1982), *Outside in....Inside Out,* Penguin, London.

Ellenberger, H. (1970), *The Discovery of the Unconscious: The History and Evolution of Dynamic Psychiatry,* Basic Books, New York.

Ernst, S and Goodison, L. (1981), *In Our Own Hands: A Book of Self-Help Therapy,* The Women's Press, London,

Evans-Pritchard, E. (1937), *Witchcraft, Oracles and Magic among the Azande,* Clarendon Press, Oxford.

Evans-Wentz, (1957), *The Tibetan Book of the Dead,* London.

Firth, R. (1975), *Symbols,* George Allen and Unwin, London.

Fosshage, J. (1987), 'New Vistas in Dream Interpretation,' in Glucksman, M. and Warner, S. (Eds.), *Dreams in New Perspective: The Royal Road Revisited,* Human Sciences Press, New York.

Fox, J. (1975), 'On Binary Categories and Primary Symbols', in Willis, Roy (ed.), *The Interpretation of Symbolism,* ASA Studies 2, Malaby Press, London.

Freud, S. (1953), *The Standard Edition of the The Complete Psychological Works of Sigmund Freud* Strachey, J. (trans. and ed.), Hogarth Press and the Institute of Psychoanalysis, London.

Freud, S. (1955), *The Interpretation of Dreams,* Basic Books, New York.

Freud, S. (1974), *Introductory Lectures on Psychoanalysis,* Pelican, London.

Fromm, E. (1955), *The Sane Society,* Holt, Rinehart and Winston, New York.

Garfield, P. (1974), *Creative Dreaming,* Ballantine Books, New York.

Gell, A. (1992), *The Anthropology of Time,* Berg, Oxford.

Gennep, A. Van (1960), *The Rites of Passage,* Trans.Vizedom, M. and Caffee, G, Routledge and Kegan Paul, London.

Glucksman, M. (1987), 'Introduction', in Glucksman, M.and Warner, S. (eds.), *Dreams in New Perspective: The Royal Road Revisited,* Human Sciences Press, New York.

Golden G and Hill, M. (1991), 'A token of loving: from melancholia to mourning', *Clinical Social Work Journal,* vol. 19, no. 1, Spring.

Gonzalez-Wippler, M. (1989), *Celibrity Book of Dreams,* Quiller Press, London.

Gouda, Y. (1991), *Dreams and Their Meanings in the Old Arab Tradition,* Vantage Press, New York.

Gregor, T. (1981), 'A content analysis of Mehinaku dreams', *Ethos* vol.9.

Hall, C. (1951), 'What people dream about', In *Scientific American,* vol. 184, no. 5.

Hall, C. and Van De Castle, R. (1966), *The Content Analysis of Dreams,* New American Library, New York.

Harris, M. (1986), *Good to Think: Riddles of Food and Culture,* Allen Unwin, London.

Hastrup, K. (1992), 'Writing ethnography: state of the art', in Okely, Judith and Callaway, Helen (eds.), *Anthropolgy and Autobiography,* ASA Monographs 29, Routledge, London.

Hartmann, E. (1984), *The Nightmare: The Psychology and Biology of Terrifying dreams,* Basic Books, New York.

Herdt, G. (1987), 'Selfhood and Discourse in Sambia Dream Sharing', in Tedlock, Barbara (Ed.), *Dreaming: Anthropological and Psychological Interpretations,* Cambridge University Press, Cambridge.

Hillman, D. (1989), 'Dreamwork and Fieldwork: Linking Cultural Anthropology and the Current Dreamwork Movement', in Ullman, Montague and Limmer, Claire (eds.), *The Variety of Dream Experience,* Aquarian Press, Wellingborough.

Hodes, M. (1989), 'Dreams reconsidered', in *Anthropology Today,* vol. 5, no. 6.

Holy, L. (1992), 'Berti Dream Interpretation' in Jedrej,M. and Shaw, Rosalind (eds), *Dreaming, Religion and Society,* Brill, Leiden.

Houston, G. (1982), *The Red Book of Gestalt,* The Rochester Foundation, London.

Jane, A, and Cooper, G. (1989), 'Working with dreams', *Nursing Times,* vol. 85, no. 21, May 24.

Jedrej, M. and Shaw, R. (1993), 'Introduction,' in Jedrej M. and Shaw, Rosalind (eds.), *Dreaming, Religion and Society in Africa,* Brill, Leiden.

Jung, C. (1948), 'General Aspects of Dream Psychology', in *Collected Works of C.G. Jung,* vol. 8, Routledge and Kegan Paul, London.

Jung, C. (1951), *Foreward to the "I Ching",*.Trans: R. Wilhelm, Routledge, London.

Jung, C. (1959a), 'Archetypes of the collective unconscious,' in *The Collected Works of C.G. Jung,* vol 9, Part 1, Routledge and Kegan Paul, London.

Jung, C. (1959b), 'Conscious, unconscious and individuation', in *The Collected Works of C.G. Jung,* vol.9, Part 1, Routledge and Kegan Paul, London.

Jung, C. (1963), *Memories, Dreams, Reflections,* Random House, New York.

Jung, C. (1964), 'Approaching the Unconscious', in *Man and his Symbols,* Aldus Books, London.

Kracke, W. (1987), 'Myths in Dreams, Thought in Images: an Amazonian Contribution to the Psychanalytic Theory of Primary Process', in Tedlock, Barbara (ed.), *Dreaming: Anthropological and Psychological Interpretations,* Cambridge University Press, Cambridge.

Kruger, S. (1992), *Dreaming in the Middle Ages,* Cambridge University Press, Cambridge.

Kubler-Ross, E. (1969), *On Death and Dying,* Macmillan, New York.

Kuper, A. (1979), 'A structural approach to dreams', *Man,* vol. 14.

Kuper, A. and Stone, A. (1982), 'The dream of Irma's injection: a structural account', *American Journal of Psychiatry,* vol. 139.

Lakoff, G. and Johnson, M. (1980), *Metaphors We Live By,* University of Chicago Press, Chicago, Ill.

Lawrence, G. (1989), 'Ventures in social dreaming: the first experience', *Changes,* vol. 7, no. 3.

Lawrence, G. (1991), 'Won from the void and formless infinite: experiences of social dreaming', *Free Associations,* vol. 2, part 2, (no. 22).

Leach, E. (1958), 'Magical Hair', *The Journal of the Royal Anthropological Institute,* vol. 88, no. 2.

Leach, E. (1970), *Lévi-Strauss,* Fontana, London.

Levine, J. (1991), 'The role of culture in the representation of conflict in dreams: a comparison of Bedouin, Irish and Israeli children', *Journal of Cross-Cultural Psychology,* vol. 22, no. 4. Dec.

Levine, S. (1981), 'Dreams of the informant about the researcher: some difficulties inherent in the research relationship', *Ethos,* vol. 9.

Lévi-Strauss, C. (1963), *'The structural study of myth',* in Basic Books, New York.

Lévi-Strauss, C. (1966), *The Savage Mind,* University of Chicago Press, Chicago, Ill.

Lévi-Strauss, C. (1970), *The Raw and the Cooked: Introduction to a Science of Mythology 1,* Johnathan Cape, London.

Lewis, I. (1977), 'Introduction' in Lewis, I. (ed.), *Symbols and Sentiments',* Academic Press, London.

Lincoln, J. (1935), *The Dream in Primitive Cultures,* William and Wilkins, Maryland.

Mackenzie, N. (1965), *Dreams and Dreaming,* Bloomsbury Books, London.

Malinowski, B. (1954), *Magic, Science and Religion,* Doubleday Anchor, New York.

Malon, D. (1989), 'Reflective use of dreams in clinical practice', *Social Casework,* vol. 70.

Mannheim, B. (1987), 'A Semiotic of Andean Dreams', In Tedlock, Barbara (ed.), *Dreaming: Anthropological and Psychological Interpretations,* Cambridge University Press, Cambridge.

Meier, F. (1966), 'Some Aspects of Inspiration by Demons in Islam', in Corbin, H. and Caillois R. (eds.), *The Dream and Human Societies,* University of California Press, Berkeley.

Miles, M. (1959), *Learning to Work in Groups,* Col.U.P., Boulder, Col.

Mogenson, G. (1990), 'The resurrection of the dead', *Journal of Analytical Psychology,* vol. 35.

Moreno, J. (1945), *Psychodrama* Vol.1. Beacon House, New York.

Needham, R. (1979), *Symbolic Classification,* Goodyear Publishing Co. Inc., Santa Monica.

Neetleton, S. (1992), *Dentistry, Pain and Power,* Open University Press, Buckingham.

Oaklander, V. (1969), *Communicating with Children,* The Center for Gestalt development, New York.

Obeyesekere, G. (1981), *Medusa's Hair,* University of Chicago Press, Chicago.

Obeyesekere, G. (1990), *The Work of Culture,* University of Chicago Press, Chicago.

Parman, S. (1991), *Dream and Culture: An Anthropological study of the Western Intellectual tradition,* Praeger, New York.

Parsifal-Charles, N. (1986), *The Dream: A Critical, Descriptive and Encyclopaedic Bibliography,* Locust Hill Press, West Cornwall, Ct.

Perls, F. (1969), *Gestalt Therapy Verbatim,* Real People Press, Lafayette, California.

Perls, F. (1971), 'Four lectures', in Fagan, J. and Shepherd, I. (eds) *Gestalt Therapy Now,* Harper Row, New York.

Preston-Shoot, M. (1987), *Effective Groupwork,* Macmillan, London.

Price-Williams, D. (1987), 'The Waking Dream in Ethnographic Perspective', In Tedlock, Barbara (ed.), *Dreaming: Anthropological and Psychological Interpretations,* Cambridge University Press, Cambridge.

Prince, P. and Hoffman, R. (1991), 'Dreams of the dying patient', *Omega,* vol. 23, no. 1.

Resnik, S. (1987), *The Theatre of the Dream,* Tavistock, London..

Rivers, W. H. R. (1918), 'Dreams and primitive culture', *Bulletin of the John Rylands library*; Library of Manchester, vol. 4.

Rowan, J. (1992), *The Transpersonal: Psychotherapy and Counselling,* Routledge, London.

Samuels, A. (1985), *Jung and the Post-Jungians,* Routledge, London.

Schutz, W. (1979), *Profound Simplicity,* Turnstone Books, London.

Seligman, C. G. (1921), 'Notes on dreams', *Sudan Notes and Records,* vol. 4.

Seligman, C. G.(1923), Type dreams: a request', *Folklore,* vol. 34.

Seligman, C.G. (1924), Anthropology and psychology: Presidential Address, *Journal of the Royal Anthropological Institute,* vol. 4.

Shohet, R. (1985), *Dream Sharing,* Turnstone Press, Wellingborough.

Sperber, D. (1975), *Rethinking Symbolism,* Cambridge University Press, Cambridge.

Stewart, K. (1951), 'Dream theory in Malaya', *Complex ,* vol. 6.

Smith, P (1980), *Group Processes and Personal Change,* Harper and Row, Cambridge.

Tedlock, B. (1987a), 'Dreaming and Dream Research', In Tedlock, Barbara (ed.), *Dreaming: Anthropological and Psychological Interpretations,* Cambridge University Press, Cambridge.

Tedlock, B. (1987b), 'Zuni and Quiche Dream Sharing and interpreting', In Tedlock, Barbara (ed.), *Dreaming: Anthropological and Psychological Interpretations,* Cambridge University Press, Cambridge.

Tuckman, B.(1965), 'Developmental sequence in small groups', *Bulletin* vol. 63, no. 6.

Turner, V. (1974), *Dramas, Fields and Metaphors,* Cornell University Press, Ithaca.

Turner, V. (1977), 'Variations on a Theme of Liminality', in Moore, S. and Myerhoff, B. (eds.), *Secular Ritual,* Van Gorcum and Co., Assen.

Tylor, E. (1871), *Primitive Culture: Researches into the Development of Mythology, Philosophy, Religion, Language, Art and Custom,* John Murray, London.

Ullman, M.D. and Zimmerman, N. (1979), *Working with Dreams,* Crucible, Wellingborough.

Ullman, M. (1989), 'Dreams and society', in Ullman, Montague and Limmer, Claire (eds.), in *The Variety of Dream Experience,* Crucible, Wellingborough.

Weisman, A. (1972), *On Dying and Denying,* Behavoural Publications, New York.

Wehr, D. (1988), *Liberating Archetypes,* Routledge, London.

Williams, S. (1984), *The Dreamwork Manual,* Acquarian Press, Wellingborough.

Wunder, D. (1993), 'Dreams as empirical data: siblings' dreams and fantasies about their disabled sisters and brothers', *Symbolic Interaction* vol. 16, no. 2.

Yalom, I. (1985), *The Theory and Practice of Group Psychotherapy,* Basic Books, New York.

Young, M. (1991), *An Inside Job: Policing and Police Culture in Britain,* Clarendon Press, New York.

Author index

Subject index

'content analysis' approach 6, 31

contextualisation 4, 51, 53-8, 83

counselling

    and use of dreams 6, 46-8, 124

Crow Indians 32

culture 1, 4, 6, 8, 9, 15-16, 31-40, 49, 51-2, 57-8, 98, 108-10, 111-20, 121-2, 123, 124

dialoguing 7

disclosure 7, 87-8, 89, 96, 97-8, 99

    spontaneous 7, 124

discussion

    use of 51, 53-8, 83

displacement 18

dramatisation 18

dream amplification 7

dream discourse 31

dream imagery

    anticipatory 20, 23, 34, 42, 43

    and cultural specificity 4, 8, 109-10

    and feminism 4, 49, 116-17, 124

    and historical development 12-17

    and idiom 102

    and metaphor 1, 3-4, 5, 7, 14, 16, 17, 19-20, 32, 36, 43, 75, 101-10

    and 'post-mortal psychical existence' 42

    progressive 42, 43

    and the social experience 19

    and symbolic construction of language 1, 4, 7, 31, 36-7, 101-10, 117

    and transformation of the personality 42

    and the unconscious experience 19

    and use of pun 102

    see also dreams, dreamwork

dream narration 31, 34

dream re-entry 51, 81-3

dream report 33

dreams

    and allegory 16

    and ambivalence 13, 41

    and children 3, 38-9, 47, 115

    communicative theory of 2, 6, 7, 33-5, 38, 39, 85, 100

    as compensatory 21, 23

    and consciousness raising 3, 115

and content analysis 31

contextualisation of 4, 51, 53-8, 83

and counselling 6, 46-81, 124

as culturally-specific metaphorical thought 1, 8, 102-7

and culture 15-16, 31-40, 51-2, 57-8, 98, 121-2, 123

'culture pattern' 6

and current life experience 1, 5, 106

and digestion 15

and ethnographic research 38-9

and expectant fathers 47-8, 124

and family therapy 2, 6, 42, 47, 48-9, 124

as future-oriented 20, 23, 34, 42, 43

'individual' 6

and infantile past 20

as integrative 5, 19-20, 113

and intentionality 118-20

interpreting 3, 4, 18, 92

and metaphor 1, 3-4, 5, 7, 14, 16, 17, 19-20, 32, 36, 43, 75, 101-10, 113, 117, 121-3

and myths 6, 30, 32-3, 116

pathogenic 6, 32

as primary process thought 18-19

and problem-solving 4, 5, 20-1, 30, 32, 43, 113

and racial prejudice 3, 115

and refugees 6, 45-6, 124

and research 2, 38-9

and responsibility 118-20

and sexual interpretation 19, 85

and social action 111-20

and social anthropology 2, 4, 5-6, 30-40, 51, 123

and social construction 4, 5, 7-8

and social context 99

and social dynamics 85

social and political perspectives of 114-20

and symbols 20, 24, 25-6, 31, 32, 36, 67, 75, 102-7, 122-3

therapeutic effect of 42-5

and the unconscious 18-19

and visions 4, 12-13

see also dream imagery, dreams, dreamwork, dreamwork groups

dreamwork

and caring professions 41-50

and children 3, 38-9, 47, 115

and consciouness raising 1, 3, 8, 115-16

cultural context of 8, 9, 32, 49, 111, 124

and empowerment 116

literature of 2-3

methods of 1, 6-7, 41-9, 51-84

movement 4, 9, 114

psychological approaches to 5, 18-29

and social action outcomes 111-20

see also dream imagery, dreams, dreamwork groups

dreamwork groups 1, 4, 7, 9, 10-11, 85-100, 115, 121-3

and bereavement 41-4

and 'coming to terms with life' 113-14

in community settings 3, 115

and conflict 6, 7, 11, 19, 88, 91-6

and decision-making 7,112

and evaluation of 7, 98-9

examples of 87-90, 103-6

and feminist perspective 49, 116-17, 124

and impact on members 111-14

and leadership 7, 10, 88, 96-7, 119-20

members of 7, 10, 85-6

methods of 1, 5, 6, 9, 11, 14, 18, 24, 26-9, 51-84, 87-90, 91, 92, 95, 98, 109, 115, 117, 123, 124

and political perspective 116-19

and power 119

and religious perspectives 16-17

and ritual structure 2, 7, 107-8, 121-3

in schools 3, 115

and self disclosure 7, 87-8, 89, 97-8

and self esteem 112-13

and social perspective 116-19

stages of 7, 86-90

and trust 7, 87, 89, 119

emplotment 121-2

ethnography 38-9

ethnopsychiatry 6, 32

expectant fathers

and dreams 47-8, 124

family therapy

and use of dreams 2, 6, 42, 47, 48-9, 124

fantasy work 87

feminism

and anima 22

and dream imagery 4

and feminist perspective 1, 49, 116-17, 124

and psychoanalysis 35

free association

use of 18

Freudian approaches 5, 6, 18-19, 31, 32, 34, 44

gender issues 89-90, 96, 99, 107, 115

gestalt methods 1, 5, 6, 11, 26-9, 44, 51, 56-7, 60, 65-75, 83, 87, 90, 91, 109, 117, 123, 124

grief 41-4

group

cohesion 96

confidentiality 87, 93-4, 98

conflict 88, 91-6

context 2, 3, 7, 85-100

evaluation 98-9

examples 87-90, 103-6

leadership 88, 92, 96-7

membership 85-6

myths 116

norms 90-1

and promotion of ritual structure 107-8

and self-disclosure 87-8, 89, 96, 97-8, 99

stages 86-90

trust 87, 89, 98, 99

see also dreamwork groups

group member Association 59-62

groupwork 1, 85-100

and culture 108

small 91

see also dreamwork groups, group

groupworkers

    issues for 119-20

Guatemala 35

guided fantasy 6, 24, 77-80, 87, 90, 92, 98, 115

Hamadsha 32

hierognosis 14

Hindu tradition 13

idiom 102

imagework 1, 14, 51, 77-80, 83, 123

'imaginal world' 14-15, 24

imaginal therapy 44

indigenous dream theory 31

intentionality 118-20

Irish children38-9

Islam 5, 13, 14-15

Israeli children 38-9

Judaic society 5, 12

Jungian perspective 5, 21-3, 34, 42

    and archetypes 5, 21-2, 58

    and collective unconscious 5

and compensation theory of dreaming 5

and transpersonal psychology 24

Kagwahi Indians 30

Kalapalo Indians 34

language 1, 4, 7, 31, 36-7, 101-10, 117

latent content 5, 18-19

learning difficulties 2, 6, 45, 124

liminality 107, 110, 121

loss 41-4

manifest content 5, 18-19, 20, 23, 33, 36

meditation 6, 9, 11, 51, 81-3, 87, 90

metaphor

    conscious 101

    and dreams 1, 3-4, 5, 7, 14, 16, 17, 19-20, 32, 36, 43, 75, 101-10, 113, 117, 121-3

    and language 101-2, 107

    and rationality 101-2

Mexico 35

myth

see also anthropological
approaches
social constructionism 2, 4, 5, 7-
8, 39, 116-17
social dreaming 8
social and political perspectives
114-20
social workers
and use of dreams 41, 44
society
and dreams 1, 3-4, 5-6, 35
sociology of dreaming 2, 8, 123
stereotypes 116, 117-19
structuralist approach 33, 62, 117
Sufi tradition 14-15
suggestion
use of 51, 52-3, 57, 90-1
supervision 6, 49-50, 124
symbol 20, 24, 25-6, 31, 32, 36,
67, 75, 102-7, 122-3
amplification 51
cultural 108-10
personal 108-10
symbolisation 18
symbolism
cultural 108-10
personal 108-10

team-building 6, 11, 49-50, 124

terminally ill people 6, 42, 45, 124
therapeutic methods 46-9
transactional analysis 84
transition 41, 42
'type dreams' 6

unconscious
collective 5, 21
cultural structuring of 15
and dreams 18-19, 41, 42,
43
nature of 5, 18, 41
social construction of 8,
111-20
and unresolved conflict 19

visions 4, 12-13
visualisation 11, 14-15, 24

women's movement 3, 115
see also feminism

Zuni tribe 35